THE *NEW* SAVORY WILD MUSHROOM

The *New* Savory Wild Mushroom

MARGARET McKENNY *and* DANIEL E. STUNTZ
Revised and enlarged by JOSEPH F. AMMIRATI

With contributions by
VARRO E. TYLER *and* ANGELO M. PELLEGRINI

University of Washington Press   SEATTLE *and* LONDON

Photographic Credits

C. Ardrey: 5, 8 top, 15-16, 23, 25, 32, 38, 41 bottom, 43-44, 47, 52, 56, 59 bottom, 63, 72, 74, 76-78, 97 bottom, 99, 111 top and bottom, 118-19, 128, 130, 132-33, 148, 153 top, 157 top, 160, 163, 166, 172 top, 183, 194, 196. *M. Beug:* 7, 17, 21 bottom, 24, 26, 28, 39, 41 top, 45, 53, 55 top and bottom, 61 bottom, 79, 90-91, 95, 121, 125, 127 bottom, 134, 150, 162, 164, 177, 179, 190. *N. Laycock:* 140. *S. Morgan:* 102, 175 top, 176, 181, 207, 213. *G. Mueller:* 69 bottom. *S. Rehner:* 123. *K. Scates-Barnhart:* 18, 21 top, 37, 42, 48, 50-51, 57, 59 top, 80-81, 83, 86, 89, 101, 106-7, 114-16, 120, 124, 127 top, 129, 131, 137, 141, 145 top, 151, 153 bottom, 154, 182, 188, 191 bottom, 193, 211. *D. Simons:* 203. *J. Spurr:* cover, 4, 8 bottom, 10 bottom, 13 top, 29, 31, 36, 49, 65 top, 66-67, 73, 75, 82, 84-85, 88, 93 top, 94, 97 top, 105, 109, 113, 135, 146-47, 157 bottom, 159 bottom, 167, 175 bottom, 180, 185 top and bottom, 186-87, 195, 197, 200-202, 204-6, 208, 210, 212, 215. *B. Woo:* 2, 10 top, 13 bottom, 14, 19, 30, 35 top and bottom, 61 top, 62, 65 bottom, 69 top, 70-71, 87, 93 bottom, 100, 103, 108, 112, 117, 138-39, 143, 145 bottom, 149, 155, 159 top, 161, 168-70, 172 bottom, 173, 178, 191 top, 192, 198.

Copyright © 1962, 1971, 1987 by the University of Washington Press
Printed in Japan by Toppan Printing Company

This book is the third edition of *The Savory Wild Mushroom* by Margaret McKenny, first published by the University of Washington Press in 1962; the second edition, revised and enlarged by Daniel E. Stuntz, was published in 1971.

Third edition first published 1987

Library of Congress Cataloging-in-Publication Data
McKenny, Margaret.
    The new savory wild mushroom.
    Rev. ed. of: The savory wild mushroom. 1971.
    Bibliography: p.
    Includes index.
    1. Mushrooms—Northwest, Pacific—Identification.
    2. Mushrooms—Northwest, Pacific—Pictorial works.
    I. Stuntz, Daniel E., 1909–   .   II. Ammirati, Joseph F.
    III. McKenny, Margaret.   Savory wild mushroom.   IV. Title.
    QK617.M423   1987   589.2'046'09795   86-28294
    ISBN 0-295-96480-4 (pbk.)

Preface

Margaret McKenny and Daniel Elliot Stuntz, authors of previous editions of *The Savory Wild Mushroom,* created the format and style of this handbook. Margaret McKenny, a naturalist and photographer in Washington State, was an enthusiastic student of fungi. Professor Stuntz was an outstanding educator at the University of Washington for over forty years, until his death in 1983. Mushrooms and other fungi were his love and his speciality.

This edition includes more information and additional mushrooms, bringing it up to date and, I hope, making it more useful. Professors Varro E. Tyler and Angelo M. Pellegrini, who wrote chapters for the second edition, also contributed to this one. The wild mushroom recipies of Margaret McKenny, present in the first and second editions, have been omitted, so that more species could be included in the handbook.

The region covered by this edition is primarily the Pacific Northwest, comprising Washington, northern Oregon, northern Idaho, and southern British Columbia. However, many of the fungi included here do occur farther south, into California, and a significant number of them occur across North America. Therefore, this handbook may be of value to almost anyone interested in mushrooms and other fungi of the United States and Canada.

The number of fungi described has been increased to 199 in this edition. New genera and species have been added to make the book more thorough; a few, not particularly common in this region, have been deleted. Edible, inedible, and poisonous mushrooms have been included, so that mushroom hunters will have a more complete presentation of the subject of wild mushrooms. Each species is illustrated in color. The text is divided on the basis of general types of fruiting bodies: boletes; chanterelles; gilled mushrooms; polypores; spine fungi; coral fungi; jelly fungi; puffballs, earthstars and false truffles; and cup fungi, helvellas, morels, false morels and truffles. Within each genus, the species are arranged alphabetically. The gilled mushrooms—the largest group—are further divided according to spore color. The common name of each fungus is given first, followed by the scientific name. Each is noted as being edible, poisonous, etc. A short bibliography is provided for those interested in pursuing further the study of fungi.

Dr. Varro E. Tyler has updated his valuable chapter on mushroom poisons, incorporating the most recent information on the subject. Dr. Angelo Pellegrini, in characteristically vigorous and delightful style, describes basic procedures for preparing, cooking, and preserving mushrooms. Several photographers and amateur mycologists contributed to the content of the book, most notably Joy Spurr, who helped select the color plates. Susan Ammirati prepared the illustration for the introduction. All those involved made their contributions to this volume as tributes to the memories of Margaret McKenny and Daniel Stuntz, hoping to pass on the enthusiasm of these two individuals for mushrooms.

J. F. Ammirati
Seattle, Washington

Contents

INTRODUCTION   ix

BOLETES   3

CHANTERELLES   25

GILLED MUSHROOMS   32
  I.   With the spore print white, pale pink, pale dingy, lilac,
       or pale cream to cream color   33
  II. With the spore print shell pink to rosey pink to
       brownish salmon   116
  III. With the spore print yellow-brown, grayish brown,
       olive-brown, cinnamon brown, rusty brown, or bright
       rust color   121
  IV. With the spore print dark reddish chocolate, purple-
       brown, brownish purple, grayish purple, purplish black,
       or black   143

POLYPORES   168

SPINE FUNGI   170

CORAL FUNGI   174

JELLY FUNGI   184

PUFFBALLS, EARTHSTARS, AND FALSE TRUFFLES   189

CUP FUNGI, HELVELLAS, MORELS, FALSE MORELS,
  AND TRUFFLES   198

MUSHROOM POISONS, by Varro E. Tyler   217

THE HUNT, THE QUARRY, AND THE SKILLET,
by Angelo M. Pellegrini   229

SELECTED BIBLIOGRAPHY   240

INDEX   242

Introduction

This book is for the mushroom hunter, to answer the recurring questions: "What is it?" and "Is it good to eat?" Anyone wishing to undertake the fascinating study of mushrooms in general should consult the bibliography at the end of the book. Many a "pothunter" has become an enthusiastic mushroom student, making the study a rewarding, lifelong hobby.

A third question—"What is the difference between a mushroom and a toadstool?"—may be answered simply. There is none. The word *toadstool* has long carried the connotation of poison. Centuries ago, toads were erroneously considered venomous and it was believed that they made a habit of sitting on mushrooms, making them poisonous. Charles McIlvaine, author of *One Thousand American Fungi,* was a scientist but pre-eminently a pothunter. He ate nearly every known fleshy mushroom and called them all "his little friends, the toadstools." He even tasted the reputedly poisonous fly amanita, with only a slight headache as a result. But don't think you should emulate him—it is truly dangerous to experiment.

Mushrooms belong to the group of organisms called fungi. Because they have no chlorophyll, the green substance that enables leafy plants in the presence of sunlight to manufacture their own food, fungi must obtain their food from living plants or animals or from their remains after death.

Some of the fungi are parasitic, existing on living plants or animals. In this division are the smuts and rusts on grains and other plants, and certain destructive mushroom growths in the forest, all of which cause great losses of crops and timber. Parasitic fungi also cause diseases such as ringworm, barber's itch, athlete's foot, and several other more serious afflictions.

A large number of fungi, including boletes, chanterelles, certain corals, many gilled mushrooms, some puffballs, and truffles, grow in association with the roots of trees and certain other woody plants. In this partnership, called a mycorrhiza (plural, mycorrhizae), the woody plant obtains water and minerals via the fungus and the fungus receives nutrients from the woody plant. Both partners require this relationship for proper growth and development. Many fungi found in forests are mycorrhizal and it is believed that the kinds of trees or shrubs and the age of the forest help to determine the kinds of fungi found there.

Many fungi are saprobic, living on decayed vegetable and animal remains. Through their work and that of various bacteria all debris returns in time to soil. Also, quite a few fungi are beneficial to people; molds, for example, which are regarded by most people as nuisances, give us many of the antibiotics so useful in modern medicine. The chance observation that certain blue-green bread and cheese molds could stop bacterial growth led to an investigation of what was stopping the growth. Enormously stimulated by the needs of war, the search for these bacterium-combating substances was soon extended to a variety of fungi, including mushrooms. Out of this research came a great number of "wonder drugs." Some of the most effective against bacteria (including several from mushrooms) are unfortunately also too poisonous to be used as medicine. The search continues, however, and new discoveries are made continually.

In this book we deal with the larger fungi that live in fields and forests. Many of them are the trophies of the mushroom gatherer and the gastronomic joy of the gourmet, while others are poisonous and to be avoided.

Mushrooms and other fungi reproduce by means of minute bodies called spores. These spores are so fine that their forms and markings can be determined only under a powerful microscope, and are produced in such vast numbers that the air is often full of them. An ordinary meadow mushroom can release nearly a million spores, and a giant puffball many more.

When one of these millions of spores settles on the proper habitat, it germinates and soon grows into a mass of threads or a felty mass called mycelium (plural, mycelia). This is the vegetative part of the mushroom, the spawn of the mushroom grower. What we call mushrooms are the fruit bodies that spring from the mycelium.

Most mushrooms have the familiar umbrella top and stem. The ordinary meadow mushroom and the commercially grown mushroom are of this type. After the spores of the meadow mushroom have

developed into the mycelium, when the temperature is between 40°
and 60° F and there have been a number of warm rains, little knobs
form on the stringy mass. These knobs grow constantly larger and
press upward until at length they show in the grass. At this stage each
has a cap and a stem and is called a button mushroom.

As it grows upward the cap expands into a spread umbrella shape,
forming the mature mushroom. On the undersurface of the cap are
numerous knifelike folds or plates called gills; these gills radiate from
the center to the edge of the cap, like spokes in a wheel. These are the
reproductive portion of the mushroom. In the meadow mushroom and
in many others, the immature gills are protected by a white mem-
brane, the partial veil, which reaches from the stem to the margin of
the cap. As the cap expands, the veil breaks, usually at the cap edge,
leaving an annulus or ring on the stem. Occasionally particles of this
veil make a fringe on the edge of the cap. The gills are now free to
release their myriad spores.

Other mushrooms, like those of the amanita group (which contains
the most deadly species), are enveloped at their early stage in a
wrapper called the universal veil. As these buttons push up into the
air, the veil breaks, leaving half in the soil in the form of a cup, or
volva, and carrying the other half on the cap, broken up into white
particles called warts, or in some species as a large felty patch.
Occasionally the volva leaves only fluffy rings on the stem.

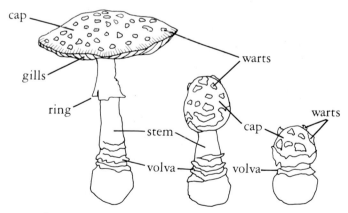

Diagram of *Amanita muscaria*

The mushrooms in this book are of two classes. In Class I are the mushrooms that bear their spores in fours on club-shaped bodies called basidia. The scientific term is basidiomycetes, from the Latin *basidium*, a club, and Greek *mykes*, a fungus or mushroom. Spore-producing basidia, besides covering the gills, also occur in tubes, whose presence is indicated by pores on the undersurface of the cap (in boletes and pore mushrooms); or on ridges, spines, or other exposed surfaces; or in the interior of fruit bodies (in puffballs and false truffles).

In Class II are the mushrooms that bear their spores in minute sacs, usually eight spores in a sac. Ascomycetes is the scientific name for these mushrooms, from *ascus*, a sac. The spore sacs are produced in cup-like structures, on cap surfaces (smooth or irregularly folded to pitted), and in the interior of truffle fruit bodies.

Most of the mushrooms of interest to the gatherer belong in Class I: the boletes, chanterelles, gilled mushrooms, pore mushrooms, spine or hedgehog mushrooms, corals, jelly mushrooms, puffballs, earth-stars, and false truffles. In Class II are the morels, helvellas, elfin-saddles, brain mushrooms, false morels, cup fungi, and truffles.

The gilled mushrooms are further divided into groups with white, pink, brown, purple-brown, or black spores. To see an example of spore color, take a meadow mushroom or one purchased fresh from a store, cut it from the stem, lay it on a piece of white paper, and cover it with a cup or bowl. Within a few hours the gills will have deposited a layer of purple-brown spores, reproducing their exact shape.

When beginning the study of mushrooms it is wise to make a spore print of every new kind of mushroom you gather. When you have decided in which spore series it belongs, check the illustrations and descriptions in the book and then decide whether you have found dinner or a reject.

But before you begin to collect mushrooms for the table, go out with an expert, if possible, for the first season. Not with a "my grandmother told me" expert, but with a scientist or experienced amateur. He or she will tell you not only how to collect mushrooms for the pot, but how to collect and prepare them if you want to send doubtful specimens to an expert for exact identification. Another excellent way to learn about mushrooms is by joining a local mushroom society. Such societies often have meetings, classes, and field trips that are particularly helpful to the beginner.

Certain tests for determining the edibility of mushrooms are based on superstition and are entirely unreliable. For example, be sure to disregard the popular belief that silver will darken when boiled with a poisonous mushroom. A newly minted dollar will still shine brightly though simmered with a destroying angel, the deadly *Amanita verna*. Disregard also the saying, "if it peels it is good to eat." The meadow mushroom peels easily, but so does the fly amanita, *Amanita muscaria*, and there are many edible mushrooms that cannot be peeled.

There are, however, several guidelines that make collecting mushrooms for food safer. Be absolutely sure of the identification of the species you are collecting for food. Be aware of edible and poisonous mushrooms that look alike. As a general rule, do not eat wild mushrooms raw. Eat only one kind of mushroom at a time and do not overindulge. The first time you sample a mushroom, eat only a small amount and observe your reaction. Often a mushroom that is perfectly safe for one individual will make another person very ill, a personal or idiosyncratic response. Learn as much as you can about the various kinds of mushroom poisoning and their symptoms. Start by reading the chapter on mushroom poisons in this book.

On your first mushroom hunt, take a sharp knife, a trowel, a roll of waxed paper, and a few small cardboard boxes for delicate specimens. Gather only fresh specimens unaffected by larvae, and be sure to dig up all of the base of the fruit body. The base is often essential for identification. Wrap each specimen in waxed paper, fold the paper vertically, and twist each end. Include if possible a button form, a half-grown, and a mature specimen. Then stand the package erect in the basket. If you are gathering for a scientist, the following simple notes which apply to gill mushrooms will be of value to the identifier:

Color and description: Type of cap, flesh, gills, and stem.

Where Found:

Remarks:

Include a spore print whenever possible.

Now, taking book and basket, start out on your adventures in the field and wood. Good hunting—and good eating!

THE *NEW* SAVORY WILD MUSHROOM

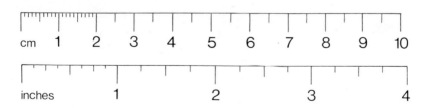

Ruler for measuring mushroom specimens and
for converting inches to centimeters

Yellow-fleshed boletus   *Boletus chrysenteron*

Boletes

Boletes are among the safest of mushrooms for the beginner, as they are easily recognized and very few of them are poisonous. Those with red pores should not be eaten, but most of the others can be tried if the usual precaution of eating only a small quantity the first time is observed. People vary in their reactions to boletes, just as to any other kind of food, and the species one person can eat with pleasure and in large quantity may prove unpalatable or even upsetting to another. Several genera of boletes, each with one or more species, are included below. The genera are in alphabetical order as are the species within each genus.

YELLOW-FLESHED BOLETUS (Edible)
Boletus chrysenteron (olive-brown spores)

Color and Description

Cap: dark brown to dull olive brown or grayish olive, plushy or velvety, cracking as it expands and showing pink or reddish color in the cracks, 2–4 inches wide; flesh yellow, may stain slightly blue where cut or bruised.

Tubes and Pores: yellow when young, becoming dingy greenish or olive greenish in old specimens, staining greenish blue where bruised.

Stem: yellow below and red above (or with these colors reversed) or yellow and more or less streaked with red, dry, sometimes grooved or scored lengthwise.

When and Where Found. Fruiting during the entire fall season and also in spring; in wooded areas of all kinds, open grassy places, or even in cultivated areas, but usually near trees.

Remarks. This is one of the commonest boletes of the Pacific Northwest, often forsaking its normal habitat in or near woods to appear in lawns, parking strips, or flower beds. It is edible, considered good by some people and rather tasteless by others; the flavor seems to be improved by drying. It is not always easy to distinguish between this bolete and Zeller's boletus, especially when the latter grows during dry weather, but for practical purposes the distinction is of little importance, as both are edible and of about the same quality.

CONIFER BOLETUS (Inedible)
Boletus coniferarum (olive-brown spores)

Color and Description

Cap: dark olive-gray to grayish brown or dark brown, at times slightly reddish or blackish, smooth to plushy, at times cracking in age, rounded to somewhat flattened, 4–12 inches wide; flesh white to pale yellow or slightly reddish in places, instantly changing to blue when cut or broken, taste bitter.

Tubes and Pores: pale yellow to yellow or olivaceous, very small, changing quickly to blue then brown when bruised.

Stem: pale yellow to yellow or olive-yellow with the very base olive-brown to blackish, sometimes reddish brown in places, stout, the base enlarged, at least the upper surface bearing a fine netlike pattern, changing to blue where handled.

When and Where Found. Fruiting in the fall season under conifers of various kinds. Most commonly found in the coastal region from Alaska to Oregon.

Remarks. This handsome bolete is too bitter to eat as is its close relative *Boletus calopus*. The latter is typically found at higher elevations under conifers, has a yellow-brown to dark brown cap that becomes deeply cracked in dry weather, and distinct pink to red areas on the stem.

Conifer boletus *Boletus coniferarum*

King boletus   *Boletus edulis*

KING BOLETUS (Edible)
Boletus edulis (olive-brown spores)

Color and Description

Cap: usually tan to some shade of brown, kidskin smooth, rounded then flat, 4–12 inches wide; flesh color same as cap color adjacent to the surface, otherwise white, not changing color or darkening slightly when broken.

Tubes and Pores: first white, then changing to yellowish green, occasionally staining yellowish when bruised, very fine; pores stuffed with white coating when very young.

Stem: white, pale dingy ivory or pale light brown, stout, sometimes very large at the base, the upper third or quarter bearing a fine but conspicuous netlike pattern.

When and Where Found. Summer, if there has been enough rain, and throughout the fall season; in spring in the Cascade Mountains, at elevations above 1,000 feet. It grows on the ground under conifers of various kinds, and sometimes is found in abundance in sandy areas adjacent to the shore of the Pacific Ocean.

Remarks. One of the best and most easily recognized of edible mushrooms. It is well known abroad as the *cep* or Steinpilz, and substantial quantities are dried and sold commercially. The stem, sometimes nearly as large as the cap, is edible if uninfected by larvae.

ADMIRABLE BOLETUS (Edible)
Boletus mirabilis (dark olive-brown spores)

Color and Description

Cap: dark maroon-brown, roughened with small, erect scales, rounded then flat, 2–5 inches wide; flesh pallid, tinged wine red just under the surface, firm, unchanging when bruised.

Tubes and Pores: yellow, then greenish, bruising deeper yellow; pores rounded to angular and fairly large.

Stem: maroon, often roughened and pitted or with a netlike pattern at the top, base enlarged.

When and Where Found. Fall, in conifer forests, on the ground or on rotten logs or rotten wood lying on the ground.

Remarks. An excellent edible species, easily identified by the dark maroon plushy cap and pitted stem and the large yellow to greenish yellow pores. Specimens attacked by a whitish mold should be discarded.

PEPPERY BOLETUS (Edible with caution)
Boletus piperatus (cinnamon-brown spores)

Color and Description

Cap: yellowish brown to cinnamon or reddish brown, rounded to somewhat flattened when older, smooth, dry to viscid, usually 3 inches or less in width; flesh yellow, often with some pinkish areas, taste strongly peppery.

Tubes and Pores: tubes yellow to reddish yellow; pores angular, relatively large, red to reddish brown; not changing to blue when bruised or exposed.

Admirable boletus *Boletus mirabilis*

Stem: cinnamon to reddish brown or pale rust color except for bright yellow base, slender, not changing to blue when bruised.

When and Where Found. Fruiting primarily in the fall season in conifer and mixed woods; sometimes common.

Remarks. *Boletus piperatus* is usually avoided because of the peppery taste. It has been reported as poisonous by some authors and by others as causing stomach upset if not cooked thoroughly. If you must try it, cook thoroughly and eat small amounts.

Peppery boletus   *Boletus piperatus*

Alice Eastwood's boletus   *Boletus pulcherrimus*

ALICE EASTWOOD'S BOLETUS (Poisonous)
Boletus pulcherrimus (brownish olive spores)

Color and Description

Cap: reddish brown, frequently with reddish tones or blushes, usually dry and somewhat suede-like, 4–10 inches wide; flesh yellow, quickly becoming blue when bruised.

Tubes and Pores: tubes yellow with dark red to brownish red pores, quickly staining blue.

Stem: pale reddish brown, lighter at the base, stout, larger at the base, 3–4 inches long, covered for most of its length with a network of fine red veins, bluing when bruised.

When and Where Found. Fall, on the ground in conifer forest at low altitudes in the Cascade and Olympic mountains.

Remarks. All boletes with red pores should be avoided, and Alice Eastwood's boletus is no exception. It is definitely poisonous, causing severe gastric upset. Until recently this species was called *Boletus eastwoodiae*. *Boletus satanas,* a similar and equally poisonous species, occurs under oaks and is more commonly found in California.

SMITH'S BOLETUS (Edible)
Boletus smithii (olive-brown spores)

Color and Description

Cap: color variable, olive, buff, or somewhat yellowish usually with some red at first, red color increasing with age, dry and velvety to nearly smooth, sometimes cracked, rounded then spreading, 2–6 inches wide; flesh pale yellow, staining blue in places, taste mild.

Tubes and Pores: yellow or pores slightly reddish at cap edge, darkening in age, staining blue when bruised or exposed; pores somewhat angular.

Stem: color somewhat variable, a mixture of yellow and red, usually with a bright red band at the apex, often narrowed at the base.

When and Where Found. Midsummer in the interior mountains, throughout the fall season into early winter in the Cascades and coastal areas.

Remarks. *Boletus smithii* has a color mixture in the cap of olive,

Smith's boletus   *Boletus smithii*

Zeller's boletus   *Boletus zelleri*

yellow and red, with red often becoming the predominate color except for the cap edge. The red band at the stem apex is helpful in distinguishing this species. The mild taste is helpful in distinguishing it from *Boletus calopus* and *Boletus rubripes*, the latter having a red stem base.

ZELLER'S BOLETUS (Edible)
Boletus zelleri (olive-brown spores)

Color and Description
Cap: dark reddish brown to nearly black, smooth, rounded then spreading, 2–4 inches wide; flesh whitish to yellow, not changing color when bruised or becoming bluish.

Tubes and Pores: olive yellow to greenish yellow or dark yellow, often becoming blue when bruised or exposed.

Stem: reddish or yellow streaked with red, white or yellowish at the base, dry.

When and Where Found. Late summer and fall, on the ground, often in Douglas fir forests or on their margins.

Remarks. This bolete is well known in the Puget Sound area and esteemed for its edible qualities. It is easily dried. Compare *Boletus chrysenteron.*

ROSY LARCH BOLETUS (Edible but not recommended)
Fuscoboletinus ochraceoroseus (reddish brown spores)

Color and Description
Cap: usually bright rosy red to pink, sometimes whitish at first, the margin at times yellowish, dry with fibrils or scales, the edge with veil fragments, rounded then flat, 3–10 inches wide; flesh yellow with a pinkish zone just below the cap surface, fairly thick, may bruise bluish.

Tubes and Pores: straw yellow or brighter yellow, finally brownish; tubes shallow; pores angular to elongated, in radial lines.

Stem: thick, yellowish, often with some red at the base, a slight netlike pattern above and fibrillose below, veil leaving a slight ring.

When and Where Found. From midsummer through fall, near or under larch, less common in the spring.

Remarks. This bolete is listed as edible in some books but tends to be bitter when cooked and therefore is not recommended for food. Other larch-associated boletes, such as *Suillus cavipes,* should be compared as well as *Suillus lakei* which is somewhat similar in appearance. The reddish brown spores of the genus *Fuscoboletinus* separate it from *Suillus,* which has cinnamon brown to yellow-brown spores. The genus *Fuscoboletinus* typically occurs with larch.

ORANGE-CAPPED BOLETUS (Edible)
Leccinum aurantiacum (yellow-brown spores)

Color and Description
Cap: bright to dark rusty red or orange-red, dry but tends to be sticky when wet or in old specimens, 2–6 inches wide; flesh white, slowly staining grayish lilac where cut.

Tubes and Pores: at first pale buff with an olive cast, then grayish brown.

Stem: pallid or white, covered with rough gray to black points; flesh white, changing color like the cap where cut or occasionally staining blue in the base.

When and Where Found. During most or all of the fall season, in conifer forests. It is often found in abundance, especially in the Cascade Mountains.

Remarks. In the Pacific Northwest there are several closely related Leccinums which differ in the color of the cap, staining of the flesh, and in microscopical features. The correct names for these different species are still to be determined, so the name *Leccinum aurantiacum* is being retained for the time being to represent this complex group of boletes. Most of these various Leccinums have probably been mistakenly collected and eaten as the orange-capped boletus, generally without ill effects. Many mushroom hunters consider Leccinums to be nearly as savory as the king boletus and they collect them in large quantity, to be frozen or dried and used between mushroom seasons. In earlier literature often called *Boletus aurantiacus.*

Rosy larch boletus   *Fuscoboletinus ochraceoroseus*

Orange-capped boletus   *Leccinum aurantiacum*

Common scaly-stemmed boletus   *Leccinum scabrum*

COMMON SCALY-STEMMED BOLETUS (Edible)
Leccinum scabrum (olive-brown spores)

Color and Description

Cap: gray brown to dull tan, often olivaceous in age, dry when young then sticky in age or when wet, usually 1–4 inches wide; flesh white, not changing color when cut or becoming slightly pinkish or brownish.

Tubes and Pores: whitish to pallid then grayish brown in age, staining or bruising yellowish or yellowish brown.

Stem: pallid to white, with brownish to blackish scales that are small and fine above and coarser below; flesh when cut usually becoming slightly pinkish in the upper portion, lower portion may have blue or reddish stains.

When and Where Found. In the Puget Sound area and elsewhere it fruits under birches that have been planted in yards, parking areas, and parks. Normally it appears in the fall season as single or scattered fruit bodies. Sometimes abundant.

Remarks. Unlike the orange-capped boletus, the common scaly-stemmed boletus is not found in forested areas unless birch is present. In California species related to *L. scabrum* grow under aspen in the mountains. In metropolitan areas where white or paper birch has been planted *L. scabrum* can sometimes produce a large number of fruit bodies over a long period of time. It is reasonably good to eat when fresh. It can be frozen or dried for later use in sauces and other dishes.

SHORT-STEMMED SLIPPERY JACK (Edible)
Suillus brevipes (cinnamon-brown spores)

Color and Description

Cap: dark wine brown to pale tan or yellowish in age, smooth, viscid to slimy when wet, 1.5–4 inches wide; flesh white to yellow, not changing color when bruised or cut.

Tubes and Pores: dull yellow becoming darker and more olivaceous in age; pores small and round.

Stem: usually 1–2 inches long, white becoming yellow; no conspicuous or well-developed glandular dots on the surface; no veil.

When and Where Found. With two- and three-needle pines, lodgepole, beach, and ponderosa pine in particular. Single, scattered, or in groups, common and often abundant, usually found in the fall season.

Remarks. The dark reddish brown cap, short pale stem lacking glandular dots when young, and the lack of a veil are the distinguishing features of this *Suillus*. In age the cap tends to become paler and somewhat streaked and the stem may develop slight glandular dots. Like most *Suillus* species, *S. brevipes* is a good but not outstanding edible. Compare the slippery jack and other kinds of *Suillus* described here. This bolete has also been called *Boletus brevipes*.

Short-stemmed slippery jack *Suillus brevipes*

Blue-staining boletus   *Suillus caerulescens*

BLUE-STAINING BOLETUS (Edible)
Suillus caerulescens (dull cinnamon-brown spores)

Color and Description

Cap: variable in color, but usually some shade of dull cinnamon or pale russet-brown in the center and dingy yellow or buff toward the margin, smooth, viscid, often with some patches or streaks on the surface, 3–6 inches wide; flesh pale yellow unchanging or becoming dingy pinkish.

Tubes and Pores: yellow when young, becoming brownish yellow with age and staining brown where bruised; typically coarse and angular.

Stem: with a fibrillose, partially or well-developed ring, above which it is yellow like the pores and below which it is sparsely to abundantly covered with matted fibrils and is dingy whitish or yellowish, often mottled with brown; flesh yellow, staining blue in the base of the stem.

When and Where Found. Throughout the fall season, in conifer forests, apparently most often associated with Douglas fir.

Remarks. This bolete looks much like Lake's boletus when the characteristic scales of the latter's cap have been wetted and matted down by rain and become tacky. *Suillus caerulescens* is edible but nor very good. It is one of the commonest boletes of the Puget Sound area and the Cascade Mountains.

HOLLOW-STALKED LARCH BOLETUS (Edible)
Suillus cavipes (olive-brown spores)

Color and Description

Cap: yellow to brown or reddish brown, dry, covered by dense fibrils or scales, edge with veil fragments, round to nearly flat, 1–4 inches wide; flesh white to yellow.

Tubes and Pores: yellow to olive; tubes shallow; pores coarse and angular to elongate and radial.

Stem: colored like cap; usually hollow in lower portion, veil leaving a slight ring.

When and Where Found. From late summer through fall, always with larch, at times very common.

Remarks. *Suillus cavipes* and *Fuscoboletinus ochraceoroseus* are both associated with larch. The former has olive-brown spores, the latter reddish brown spores. In addition the hollow stem and yellow to brown, scaly, dry cap are distinguishing features of *S. cavipes*. Reported to be an excellent edible.

Hollow-stalked larch boletus   *Suillus cavipes*

DOTTED-STALKED SLIPPERY JACK (Edible)
Suillus granulatus (dull cinnamon spores)

Color and Description

Cap: pale buff streaked and mottled with cinnamon brown, then brown all over, smooth, viscid, slimy when wet, 2–4 inches wide; flesh whitish to pale yellow, not changing color where bruised or cut.

Tubes and Pores: pallid, pores beaded with droplets of slimy liquid when young, becoming yellow and spotted with brown, staining dingy cinnamon where bruised.

Stem: bright yellow at top, white or pallid elsewhere, covered with pinkish tan to purplish brown viscid glandular dots.

When and Where Found. Fall, and sometimes spring if there is enough moisture; associated with pines.

Remarks. There are several boletes similar enough in general appearance to *Suillus granulatus* to be collected and eaten as slippery jacks, seemingly without any ill consequences. One of these, *Suillus punctatipes,* deserves special mention, being fairly common in the Pacific Northwest. It is associated with Douglas fir and other conifers and differs from *S. granulatus* by its purplish brown cap and coarser pores, which are arranged in conspicuously radiating lines.

Dotted-stalked slippery jack   *Suillus granulatus*

Lake's boletus *Suillus lakei*

LAKE'S BOLETUS (Edible)
Suillus lakei (yellow-olive spores)

Color and Description

Cap: reddish to reddish brown or yellow, rough and scaly, yellow flesh showing between the tufted scales, first rounded then flat, 2–6 inches wide; flesh yellow, thick, unchanging or pinkish where exposed.

Tubes and Pores: yellow, brownish to reddish when bruised; pores typically coarse and angular.

Stem: yellow at apex, fibrillose and about the color of the cap below a whitish annular zone, in age sometimes bluish in base.

When and Where Found. From early to late fall, on the ground usually near Douglas fir, often growing in quantity under young Douglas fir trees.

Remarks. Edible, but rather coarse and tasteless. The brown, rough-fibered top is quite distinctive but compare *Suillus caerulescens*. Sometimes called *Boletus lakei* or *Boletinus lakei* in the literature.

SLIPPERY JACK (Edible)
Suillus luteus (cinnamon-brown spores)

Color and Description

Cap: yellow-brown to red-brown or sometimes with a purplish brown cast, smooth, slimy when wet, shinning and appearing varnished when dry, 2–4 inches wide; flesh white to pale yellow, not changing color where bruised.

Tubes and Pores: whitish to pale yellow at first, then dull greenish yellow, not changing color where bruised; the edges have tiny viscid glandular dots that turn dark brown with age.

Stem: with a flaring to bandlike membranous or feltlike ring whose outer surface is covered with red-brown or purplish brown slime, surface yellow and covered with small viscid glandular dots above the ring, felted or matted-fibrillose and dingy white or streaked with brownish slime below the ring; flesh pale yellow or whitish, not changing color where bruised.

When and Where Found. Fall, associated with various kinds of pines, at times found in metropolitan areas where pines have been planted, and perhaps spruce; not as common as the other slippery jacks, (*Suillus granulatus* and *S. brevipes*).

Remarks. Edible and good. The slimy surface of the cap should be removed before cooking. Also called *Boletus luteus*. *Suillus umbonatus,* a similar slippery jack, can be found under lodgepole pine and beach pine in coastal areas, and with lodgepole pine in the mountains. It has large, radially arranged pores, a distinct, viscid, pale watery brown ring, and a viscid cap that is yellow to brown and then develops olive tones in age. *Suillus subolivaceus,* described below, is also similar.

OLIVE-CAPPED BOLETUS (Edible)
Suillus subolivaceus (dull cinnamon spores)

Color and Description

Cap: olive-yellow to olive or olive-brown, usually darker in the center, slimy-viscid when wet, sometimes streaked with black radiating lines under the viscid layer, smooth, 2–4 inches wide; flesh whitish to yellowish or with a grayish olive tinge, not changing color or slightly pinkish when exposed.

Slippery jack   *Suillus luteus*

Olive-capped boletus   *Suillus subolivaceus*

Tubes and Pores: yellowish to pale grayish buff or grayish olive, beaded with viscid droplets when young, becoming dingy yellow or brownish yellow, not changing color or becoming brownish where bruised, the droplets often drying black.

Stem: girded by a conspicuous bandlike ring fastened to the stem at its middle, with its upper and lower edges free and covered on the outside with brown or olive slime, yellow above the ring and dingy white below, but densely covered everywhere with viscid, glandular pinkish brown dots which become black.

When and Where Found. Fall, most frequently under western white pine.

Remarks. In spite of its unprepossessing appearance, this bolete is edible, but rather poor. It somewhat resembles one of the slippery jacks (*Suillus luteus*), but can be distinguished by the black viscid dots on the stem below the ring and by its peculiar bandlike or collarlike ring. The black dots on the stem are sometimes so numerous that they run together in a continuous slimy patch. The slime from them and from the surface of the cap stains one's fingers brown.

Suillus sibiricus is another species associated with white pine. It has a viscid yellow cap with reddish brown plaques toward the margin and cottony veil tissue at the edge. The pores are large, radially arranged, and yellow. The stem is basically yellow, moist to viscid, and develops brownish glandular dots; normally there is no ring. All parts tend to stain wine color or brown and the sticky stem will stain one's fingers black. Similar to the eastern *S. americanus*.

WOOLLY-CAPPED BOLETUS (Edible)
Suillus tomentosus (dark olive-brown spores)

Color and Description

Cap: entirely covered at first with small, matted-hairy or woolly, gray or brownish gray scales that become separated as the cap expands, revealing the underlying viscid, yellow to pale orange-yellow cap surface, hence the cap is grayish brown at first, then yellow to orange-yellow, spotted with grayish brown as it gets older, 2–4 or up to 6 inches wide; flesh pale yellow, turning blue where cut or bruised.

Woolly-capped boletus *Suillus tomentosus*

Tubes and Pores: dark cinnamon brown when young, becoming yellow in older caps, changing to blue where bruised.

Stem: yellow or orange-yellow, covered all over with abundant tiny, viscid, glandular dots that become brownish or darker; flesh yellow, staining blue where cut or bruised.

When and Where Found. Fall, under conifers, particularly under pines; often abundant in the Cascade Mountains. It is one of the Pacific Northwest's commoner species.

Remarks. Edible, but rather poor. Cap, stem, and scales are all variable in color, and in addition the scales may disappear completely, leaving the cap smooth. The scales become sticky when wet, and in wet weather the surface of the cap is almost slimy. This bolete is best recognized by the dark brown color of its young pores and the blue staining of the flesh and tubes: no other bolete in the Pacific Northwest has just this combination of features.

The dark boletus   *Tylopilus pseudoscaber*

THE DARK BOLETUS (Edibility unknown)
Tylopilus pseudoscaber (dark reddish brown, dark chocolate spores)

Color and Description

Cap: olive-brown to very dark brown or black, dry, dull, velvety, rounded then spreading, 2–6 inches wide; flesh white or pink when cut, white areas staining weakly blue then pinkish to reddish brown or dull brown, staining waxed paper blue-green.

Tubes and Pores: dark brown to black, often staining bluish then dark brown when bruised.

Stem: dark brown, like the cap, except for the whitish base, equal or with a club-shaped base; ridged lengthwise and often with a raised netlike pattern; staining reddish to dark brown or black when bruised, scattered areas staining blue.

When and Where Found. Late summer into the winter season on the Pacific coast and in the interior mountains. Growing in woods of mixed conifers and hardwoods or in coniferous forests.

Remarks. Easily recognized by the overall dark brown to dull black color except for the base of the stem which is whitish. The blue staining reaction of the flesh when exposed and the blue staining of waxed paper are helpful distinguishing features. *Boletus olivaceobrunneus* is another name that has been used for this species in the past.

Chanterelles

Chanterelles, as differentiated from gilled mushrooms, have a fertile surface of blunt-edged veins rather than sharp-edged, bladelike gills on the undersurface of the cap. Also, some of them are characterized by their trumpet- or vase-shaped cap. *Cantharellus cibarius* is the best known species and the one most readily recognized and collected by beginners. Only one species, *Gomphus floccosus,* is considered toxic; see the remarks following its description. The genera are in alphabetical order as are the species within each genus.

YELLOW CHANTERELLE (Edible)
Cantharellus cibarius (yellowish spores)

Color and Description

Cap: golden to dark egg yellow, sometimes shaded with tan, smooth, at first rounded, then upturned, center more or less sunken and margin ruffled, 2–5 inches wide; flesh solid white, taste mild to spicey, odor apricot-like or mildly fragrant.

Yellow chanterelle   *Cantharellus cibarius*

Fertile surface: pale yellow to orange; shallow, blunt-edged ridges, with interlacing veins, running down the stem.

Stem: yellow to whitish, sometimes bruising orange, usually smooth, often larger at the base, 3–5 inches long.

When and Where Found. Late summer to late fall, often under Douglas firs, hemlock, or spruce, in old or second-growth forests.

Remarks. One of the best-known and best-liked mushrooms of the West and elsewhere. Tender and of good quality, often growing in great abundance year after year in the same woods. It usually is smaller than the woolly chanterelle, and has no woolly red scales in the center. A similar species, *Cantharellus subalbidus,* is described below. Also compare *Hygrophoropsis aurantiaca,* a gilled mushroom sometimes confused with the yellow chanterelle.

FUNNEL-SHAPED CHANTERELLE (Edible)
Cantharellus infundibuliformis (yellow or creamy yellow spores)

Color and Description

Cap: brownish gray or brown or dingy tan, with arched margin

Funnel-shaped chanterelle   *Cantharellus infundibuliformis*

when young, then funnel-shaped, developing a hole in the center opening into the hollow stem, 1–2 inches wide; flesh yellowish, thin. *Fertile Surface:* grayish yellow to yellow, of blunt-edged, veinlike ridges, often forked and connected by crossveins.

Stem: yellow or yellowish tan, smooth, hollow, 3–4 inches long.

When and Where Found. Late summer and fall, in boggy soil in conifer forests, frequently under the edges of rotting logs. Often abundant in the Cascade and Olympic mountains at low elevations.

Remarks. Edible, but the flavor is not particularly pleasing to most people. A very closely related chanterelle, *Cantharellus tubaeformis,* differs principally in having a white spore print. What has been referred to in the Pacific Northwest for years as *C. infundibuliformis* is, according to mycologists from Europe and the eastern United States, probably a group of species differing only slightly from one another. To the mushroom hunter and mycophagist who has collected and eaten the whole complex many times, such distinctions are of no particular importance.

WHITE CHANTERELLE (Edible)
Cantharellus subalbidus (white spores)

Color and Description

Cap: white overall but staining rusty yellow to orange-brown where injured, smooth or slightly scaly in age, flattened to somewhat sunken towards the center, edge turned down or elevated and often lobed to wavy, 2–6 inches wide; flesh solid, very firm and thick, white with a tendency to stain yellow where bruised.

Fertile Surface: white to grayish white becoming cream colored and stained yellow to orange where bruised, shallow, blunt-edged ridges, with interlacing veins, running down the stem almost to the base.

Stem: white and staining yellow to orange or brownish where bruised, especially at base, thick, stout, up to 3 inches long.

When and Where Found. Single or in groups under conifers; fall and winter seasons, often abundant.

Remarks. The white chanterelle often occurs with the yellow chanterelle and is classified as an excellent edible. Its large size and firm texture add to its attraction for the pothunter.

White chanterelle   *Cantharellus subalbidus*

PIG'S EAR GOMPHUS (Edible)
Gomphus clavatus (ocher to ocher-brown spores)

Color and Description

Cap: seal brown or tan, often shaded purple, smooth, irregular on margin, more or less sunken in the center, often in overlapping clusters, 5 or more inches wide; flesh white to grayish.

Fertile Surface: purplish to purplish brown or tan, shaded deep purple at the base of shallow, wrinkled blunt-edged ridges or veins running far down the stem.

Stem: brown or purple, forming part of the cap, sometimes fused with adjacent stems, often in dense clusters, 5–6 inches long.

Pig's ear gomphus   *Gomphus clavatus*

When and Where Found. Late summer and fall, in old-growth Douglas fir forests, usually in the Cascade and Olympic mountains.

Remarks. An excellent edible fungus, considered by some to be the best of the chanterelles. Delicious when sliced and fried with meat.

WOOLLY CHANTERELLE (Edible but not recommended)
Gomphus floccosus (ocher spores)

Color and Description

Cap: yellowish white to orange, the center roughened with orange to orange-red woolly scales, center sunken to funnel-shaped, 3–4 inches wide; flesh cream-white.

Woolly chanterelle *Gomphus floccosus*

Fertile Surface: cream-white to buff or yellowish, shallow wrinkles or blunt-edged ridges with many interlacing veins running far down the stem.

Stem: cream-white to yellowish, stout, 5–10 inches in long; whole mushroom sometimes 16 inches high.

When and Where Found. Early to late fall, usually in old-growth Douglas fir forests.

Remarks. The orange to orange-red woolly center and its size distinguish *Gomphus floccosus* from the safe and delicious yellow chanterelle. This beautiful vase-shaped mushroom, which in the past has been classed as edible, causes indigestion in some people. Recently some compounds have been found in the woolly chanterelle that might be harmful to the liver. It would be advisable, therefore, not to eat the woolly chanterelles, at least not frequently or in large quantity. *Gomphus kauffmanii* should also be avoided. It is somewhat larger than *G. floccosus,* has coarse, tan to light olive brown scales on the funnel-shaped cap and a yellow-buff fertile surface that is wrinkled or forms shallow pores.

Clustered blue chanterelle *Polyozellus multiplex*

CLUSTERED BLUE CHANTERELLE (Edible)
Polyozellus multiplex (white spores)

Color and Description

Cap: deep purple violet-black or blue-black to blue, fan- to spoon-shaped, flat or somewhat sunken in the center, edge irregularly lobed or wavy, 1–4 inches wide; flesh thick, blue-black.

Fertile Surface: purplish to pale violet, shallow, forming a veined to netted pattern or porelike.

Stem: violet or purple-black, usually fused or grown together, solid or sometimes hollow, brittle, 1–2 inches long.

When and Where Found. Occurring in compact clusters or masses on the ground under conifers, often spruce or fir; more frequently found at higher elevations.

Remarks. The clustered blue chanterelle is not particularly common but when found usually there will be enough for one or more meals. It is considered edible and good. Compare with pig's ear gomphus.

Gilled Mushrooms

Gilled mushrooms form by far the largest group of fungi of interest to the mushroom hunter. They include the most dangerous poisonous species one is likely to encounter, as well as some of the best edible ones. Anyone attempting to identify gilled mushrooms must be familiar with their structure, which is explained in the introduction. Use the utmost caution in testing the edibility of forms you do not positively recognize.

Since the beginner should always try to get a spore print when investigating an unfamiliar mushroom, the gilled mushrooms are here grouped by spore color: white and pale spore prints begin on the next page; pink and reddish spore prints on page 116; yellow to brown spore prints on page 121; and dark brown to black spore prints on page 143. Within those groups the mushrooms are listed alphabetically by genus and by species within each genus.

Warted amanita   *Amanita aspera*

I. Gilled mushrooms with the spore print white, pale pink, pale dingy lilac, or pale cream to cream color. In some species of *Russula* and *Lactarius* the spore print is yellow or ocher.

WARTED AMANITA (Poisonous)
Amanita aspera (white spores)

Color and Description

Cap: very dark brown, with many soft, fragile, gray or yellowish gray warts, 3–5 inches wide; flesh white or pale yellowish white.

Gills: white, or sometimes pale yellow, free from the stem.

Stem: yellow above the ring, grayish yellow to brownish gray below, ring ample, yellow on its upper surface, gray or yellowish gray beneath, usually with felty gray or yellow patches along the edge; base of stem with a bulb on which a few irregular zones or warts of grayish veil remnants form the volva.

When and Where Found. Fall, on the ground in conifer forests.

Remarks. This amanita looks like the dark brown forms of *Amanita pantherina,* but its ring and the warts on its cap are not white, as are those of the panther amanita, and it has a different type of volva. It should be regarded as poisonous and avoided.

CAPPED AMANITA (Edible with caution)
Amanita calyptrata (white spores)

Color and Description

Cap: yellow-orange, darker brownish orange in young stages, rounded then broadly expanded, smooth, viscid, etched lines on margin, 2–12 inches wide, usually capped by a large, felty, white portion of the universal veil; flesh white, soft.

Gills: creamy white or yellowish, at first covered with a white veil which, on breaking, forms a ring on the stem.

Stem: creamy white, rather short, rising from a large, white, felty cup, the remains of the universal veil.

When and Where Found. Fall, in mixed woods or on their margins.

Remarks. This is an edible amanita, but should be avoided by the collector, for fear of confusion with other poisonous amanita species. It is common in southern Oregon, California, and the vicinity of Victoria, B.C., but is rather rare in Washington.

JONQUIL AMANITA (Poisonous)
Amanita gemmata (white spores)

Color and Description

Cap: yellow, smooth, tacky when wet, with scattered white warts, 3–4 inches wide; flesh white.

Gills: white or very pale ivory, free from the stem.

Stem: white, usually with a bulbous base, ring white, thin but ample, volva with a distinct upper rim that is free from the bulb.

When and Where Found. Fall, usually under Douglas fir and other conifers; sometimes abundant at lower elevations in the Puget Sound area.

Remarks. The yellow cap distinguishes typical specimens of this amanita from typical specimens of the panther amanita, intermediate colors can be found. This indicates that the jonquil amanita may be poisonous. Put it on your "poison list," since it can be confused with pale forms of *Amanita pantherina*.

FLY AMANITA (Poisonous)
Amanita muscaria (white spores)

Color and Description

Cap: brilliant red or orange, orange in the center shading to yellow at the margin, or entirely yellow, first rounded then flattened and somewhat upturned, with cream-white or white particles or warts covering the surface and often adhering to the margin, 3–12 inches wide; flesh white.

Gills: white or cream-white, usually free from the stem, first covered with the white partial veil which, on breaking, forms a ring on the stem, portions sometimes adhering to the edge of the cap.

Stem: white, larger at the base, which shows concentric rows of fluffy white scales, the remains of the volva or wrapper.

Capped amanita *Amanita calyptrata*

Jonquil amanita *Amanita gemmata*

Fly amanita *Amanita muscaria*

When and Where Found. Occasionally in spring or summer, but most abundant in late autumn, on the ground in conifer forests or mixed woods, or on their edges, sometimes in bushes near open fields.

Remarks. This is the mushroom so often pictured in European fairy tales. It is called "fly amanita" because it is thought a decoction made from it kills flies. It is definitely dangerous but fortunately it is quite easy to recognize; the bright red, orange, or yellow cap with its white warts is in itself a conspicuous warning for even the most unwary collector. It also comes in forms with white or brown caps, and the veil may be a striking yellow instead of the more typical white.

DESTROYING ANGEL (Deadly poisonous)
Amanita ocreata (white spores)

Color and Description
Cap: white at first then pinkish to buff at the center and often buff on the margin with age, moist to viscid, smooth, first rounded then flattened, 2–5 inches wide; flesh white.

Gills: white, usually free from the stem, first concealed with a veil which on breaking forms a white, conspicuous ring on the stem which may collapse and disappear in age.

Stem: white, staining pale brown when bruised, 3–8 inches long, base in a loose cup or volva, the remains of the universal veil.

When and Where Found. Solitary or in groups, usually under oak, often live oak; known in California and southern Oregon but watch for this species in other areas. Usually fruiting winter to early spring, January into April.

Remarks. This is a deadly poisonous mushroom, as are the other destroying angels, such as *Amanita verna* and *Amanita virosa.* These and the death cup, *Amanita phalloides,* are less common in the Puget Sound area than farther south, particularly in California, where a number of poisonings occur each year.

Amanita verna, a pure white amanita, similar in size and stature to *Amanita ocreata,* has been found in the Pacific Northwest in Douglas fir forests, and it or a close relative has caused at least one severe poisoning. *Amanita verna* has been collected near Vancouver, Washington, and around Lake Kachess. Its probable presence elsewhere in Washington and the occurrence of *Amanita ocreata* in Oregon point up the necessity for extreme caution in considering any large, white or whitish mushroom for the table. Look for the telltale features of the destroying angel group: free gills, well-developed ring, and a membranous, saclike volva. Chances of recovery from poisoning by the destroying angel and death cup can be less than fifty percent.

Destroying angel   *Amanita ocreata*

PANTHER AMANITA (Poisonous)
Amanita pantherina (white spores)

Color and Description

Cap: pale tan to dark brown, viscid, decorated with white or cream-white particles or warts, first rounded then flat, 4–12 inches wide; flesh white.

Gills: white, first covered with a partial veil which, on breaking, forms a ring on the stem.

Stem: white, base enlarged, rising from a close fitting cup or volva with a distinct, rolled edge; young fruit body completely covered with the universal veil.

When and Where Found. Spring and fall, or throughout the winter in mild seasons, on the ground, conifer or mixed forests, often under Douglas fir trees, especially abundant in the Puget Sound area.

Remarks. The panther amanita is so named because of the panther-like spots on the cap. In the Pacific Northwest it has caused more cases of poisoning than any other mushroom. Its characteristics should be carefully memorized in order that it may be avoided. Remember: white warts on a brown or tan cap, white gills, and a distinct close-fitting cup at the base of the stem—these are danger signals.

Panther amanita   *Amanita pantherina*

DEATH CUP (Deadly poisonous)
Amanita phalloides (white spores)

This species differs from the destroying angels only in the color of the cap, which is greenish yellow, grayish olive, or brownish rather than pure white. The stem is white or tinted with cap colors. It is equally poisonous, and is said to account for the majority of fatal cases of mushroom poisoning in Europe. *Amanita phalloides* has been found growing in Seattle, and may occur elsewhere in Washington. It also occurs in southern Oregon and northern California, and might eventually find its way into other areas. In California, it and *Amanita ocreata* cause a significant number of poisonings with some fatalities each year. Be on the lookout for it and be familiar with its characteristic features: the smooth, greenish yellow cap, free white gills, ample white ring, and membranous, saclike volva.

Death cup   *Amanita phalloides*

PURPLE-BROWN AMANITA (Possibly poisonous)
Amanita porphyria (white spores)

Color and Description
Cap: grayish brown with a subtle purplish case, with a few fragile gray patches of veil tissue, 3–4 inches wide; flesh white.

Gills: white, usually free, sometimes just touching the top of the stem.

Stem: with a large, conspicuous bulb at the base that is often split into broad lobes, bearing a few gray felty patches of volva that are easily obliterated, white or pale gray above the thin, gray ring, decorated below the ring with gray or purplish gray patches and zones.

When and Where Found. Fall, in conifer woods at all elevations. Not rare, but it tends to occur one specimen at a time, scattered over a large area.

Remarks. The purplish tinge that gives this amanita its name is not always well developed. The large bulb, gray ring, and gray patches on the stem are its distinguishing marks. Whether it is poisonous is not known with certainty. Assume that it is poisonous and avoid it completely.

WOODLAND AMANITA (Poisonous)
Amanita silvicola (white spores)

Color and Description
Cap: white, dry, often fluffy with remains of the universal veil, first rounded then flat, 3–4 inches wide; flesh white, soft, little odor.

Gills: white, first hidden with delicate partial veil which, on breaking, sometimes forms a slight ring on the stem.

Stem: white, usually short, larger at the base, showing fluffy remains of volva or wrapper, but no distinct cup.

When and Where Found. Fall, on the ground in conifer forests or on their edges.

Remarks. Although this pure white amanita is quite common in the Puget Sound area, there are no reports concerning its edibility. It is advisable not to experiment with any of the amanita group.

Purple-brown amanita *Amanita porphyria*

Woodland amanita *Amanita silvicola*

Smith's amanita   *Amanita smithiana*

SMITH'S AMANITA (Poisonous)
Amanita smithiana (white spores)

Color and Description

Cap: white to off-white, moist to slightly viscid, often with patches or warts of the universal veil which is white but often discolors slightly buff or brown, first rounded then flattened, 3–6 inches wide; flesh white, odor strong and unpleasant like chlorine.

Gills: white, slightly attached to the stem then free, first hidden with delicate veil which, on breaking, sometimes forms a slight ring on the stem or collapses entirely.

Stem: white, 3–6 inches long, tapered upward, base enlarged, at times rooting; universal veil forming white warts and patches above and one or more rings of white tissue on the base, the latter often inconspicuous and lost in age.

When and Where Found. On the ground in conifer woods during the fall season. It appears to be more common in the coastal forests.

Remarks. Smith's amanita and the woodland amanita are fairly common in the Pacific Northwest extending into California. *Do not eat any white amanitas.* There are several cases of poisoning reported for *Amanita smithiana* and there may well be other similar-looking toxic species in the Puget Sound area and elsewhere in the West.

SHEATHED AMANITA (Edible with caution)
Amanita vaginata (white spores)

Color and Description

Cap: gray-brown to gray, bell-shaped then flat, deep lines on edge of cap, 1–4 inches wide; flesh white.

Gills: white, free from stem.

Stem: whitish, slender, 3–4 inches long, without ring; base deep in the soil, covered with the remains of the universal veil, which completely envelops the young mushroom.

When and Where Found. Spring and fall, usually in conifer woods or on their margin.

Remarks. Though *Amanita vaginata* is not poisonous, it should be avoided because of the danger to beginners of confusing it with amanitas that are poisonous. The color of the cap varies considerably, but all forms are well marked by the large saclike volva and the absence of a ring on the stem.

Sheathed amanita *Amanita vaginata*

Shaggy-stalked armillaria   *Armillaria albolanaripes*

SHAGGY-STALKED ARMILLARIA (Edibility uncertain)
Armillaria albolanaripes (white spores)

Color and Description

Cap: yellow with brownish center, with brownish scales and fibrils radiating from the center, edge may be whitish, slightly viscid when moist, rounded to flattened with a central knob, 2–5 inches wide; flesh white with yellow near the cap.

Gills: white to yellow, attached but deeply notched at the stem and sometimes appearing nearly free.

Stem: 1–3 inches long, up to one inch thick, white above the white ragged cottony ring, below the ring sheathed by white to yellowish ragged scales often in concentric zones.

When and Where Found. Solitary or in groups, on the ground, usually under conifers. Fruits in the summer and fall seasons in the Pacific Northwest, in warmer areas of California found into February.

Remarks. This is a fairly common armillaria in some seasons. A similar species is *Armillaria luteovirens,* which has a more conspicuously scaly cap which is yellow overall. No cases of poisoning are reported for either species but they are still of uncertain edibility.

HONEY MUSHROOM (Edible with caution)
Armillariella mellea (white spores)

Color and Description

Cap: honey-colored, varying through shades of tan to dark brown, first rounded then flattened with slightly upturned margin that shows an etching of fine lines, surface often with hair-like scales, 3–6 inches wide; flesh tan or brownish.

Gills: pale cream to dull tan, often powdered with white spores, first covered with a white veil.

Stem: tan or brownish with a ring formed by remains of the veil, somewhat larger at base, usually in dense clusters.

When and Where Found. Early to late fall, in the open or in the forest, at the base of or on dead trees and logs, sometimes in a wound in a live tree.

Remarks. Very common in the woodland, of good flavor but

Honey mushroom   *Armillariella mellea*

rather tough and coarse. Use only the caps; the stems are tough and fibrous. It must be cooked thoroughly. Some individuals develop stomach upset when eating it, so use caution.

This mushroom produces black, cordlike strands or rhizomorphs (meaning rootlike) that sometimes can be seen attached to the base of the stem. These black strands may penetrate the roots of trees or shrubs, and once inside, they can girdle the root, or even move up and girdle the trunk, killing the invaded plant. This activity has earned the fungus another popular name, "shoestring root rot," because the rhizomorphs look like black shoelaces.

Few mushrooms are as variable in size, color, surface of the cap, or color and texture of the ring as is *Armillariella mellea*. A description of all the variations would fill two or three pages. It is easy to see why it takes a long time to recognize the honey mushroom in all its forms.

SWOLLEN-STALKED CATATHELASMA (Edible)
Catathelasma ventricosa (white spores)

Color and Description

Cap: off white to grayish, dry, smooth, rounded to broadly rounded, large, 3–6 inches wide; flesh thick, hard, white, taste somewhat unpleasant.

Gills: close together or somewhat spaced, extending down stem, often forked, whitish to buff; covered by a double veil at first which, on breaking, forms a double ring on the stem.

Stem: 2–5 inches long, very thick, tapered downward, white above the double, felty ring, below the ring whitish, tinted grayish or dull yellow-brown from an outer sheathing veil.

When and Where Found. Fruits in the summer and fall seasons. Solitary or several together on the ground under conifers; in coastal areas as well as in the mountains.

Remarks. This and a similar species, *Catathelasma imperialis,* are among the largest of the gill mushrooms in the west. They are often infrequent but may be locally common in some years. *Catathelasma imperialis* is larger, 6–16 inches wide, than *Catathelasma ventricosa,* has a brownish cap that is sticky when moist, and normally is found in the mountains of the interior.

Swollen-stalked catathelasma   *Catathelasma ventricosa*

WHITE-STRANDED CLITOCYBE (Edibility unknown)
Clitocybe albirhiza (white spores)

Color and Description

Cap: watery pale buff beneath a thin, whitish coating at first, watery brown in age or when water soaked, pale buff or pinkish buff in dry weather or when faded, rounded at first then centrally depressed to somewhat funnel-shaped, 1–4 inches wide; flesh thin to moderately thick, colored like the surface, odor and taste somewhat disagreeable.

Gills: white then pale buff, squarely attached or slightly running down the stem, close together, narrow to broad, at times forked, often with interconnecting veins.

Stem: usually 1–3 inches long, fibrous and tough, colored like the cap, the base with a dense mass of white strands embedded in duff or needles; hollow in age.

When and Where Found. Spring and early summer, at times common. Scattered or in groups, under conifers at higher elevations,

White-stranded clitocybe   *Clitocybe albirhiza*

usually near the edge of melting snow banks or soon after snow has receded.

Remarks. This is a species of the western mountains often encountered by persons collecting spring mushrooms. The general color, white strands on the base of the stem, and habitat, near melting snow banks, are helpful identifying characteristics. The edibility of this species is unknown. It is one of a large group of species, some of which are poisonous, so it should not be experimented with.

SMOKY BROWN CLITOCYBE (Edibility uncertain)
Clitocybe avellaneialba (white spores)

Color and Description

Cap: dark grayish brown or dark brown tinged with olive, flat or with slightly depressed center, with a rounded, often shallowly ribbed margin in mature caps, smooth, moist, 3–6 inches wide; flesh white or tinged with the color of the cap, without special odor.

Smoky brown clitocybe   *Clitocybe avellaneialba*

Gills: white or pallid, sometimes cream color in age, running down the stem, narrow.

Stem: same color as the cap but usually paler, smooth, dry, with club-shaped base.

When and Where Found. Fall, on the ground in conifer hardwood or mixed woods.

Remarks. This handsome clitocybe is native to the Pacific Coast, and often common in western Washington and Oregon. There have been reports of people eating it, but not enough to establish its edibility beyond doubt.

SWEAT-PRODUCING CLITOCYBE (Poisonous)
Clitocybe dealbata var. *sudorifica* (white to cream spores)

Color and Description
Cap: white to grayish, sometimes with pinkish tones, first

Sweat-producing clitocybe   *Clitocybe dealbata* var. *sudorifica*

rounded, at length upturned with depressed center, 1–2 inches wide; flesh whitish to watery buff, thin.

Gills: whitish to pale buff, close together, fine, running down the stem.

Stem: whitish to buff, short, tough, 2–3 inches long.

When and Where Found. From early fall until after frost, on the ground, usually in the open, in fields with meadow mushrooms, and on lawns, where it occasionally forms rings.

Remarks. While not deadly, this mushroom produces quite disagreeable cases of profuse sweating as well as other characteristic symptoms. The poisonous substance it contains is muscarine (see the chapter on mushroom poisons). This clitocybe should be carefully distinguished from the true fairy ring mushroom which grows in similar places. The latter has broad cream-white gills which do not run down the stem.

CROWDED WHITE CLITOCYBE (Poisonous)
Clitocybe dilatata (white spores)

Color and Description
Cap: gray becoming whitish with areas of watery buff, chalky white when dry or in dry weather, round then flattened to somewhat depressed centrally, edge usually enrolled, margin irregular, usually deformed from pressure of adjacent caps, 1–6 inches wide; flesh moderately thick at the center, gray to white.

Gills: whitish to slightly yellowish, buff or pinkish buff, squarely attached or running down the stem, close together or crowded together, occasionally forked.

Stem: colored like the cap, somewhat stained, darker with bruising, usually 2–5 inches long, typically compressed, often curved, central to somewhat off center, at times the bases of several fused.

When and Where Found. From late summer into the winter depending on the location and the year. In clusters or many together in one area, in the open on bare soil or under low vegetation, frequently seen on the edges of roads.

Remarks. This clitocybe is usually found in dense clusters on road shoulders and is frequently seen by collectors in the Pacific Northwest. It is reported to contain muscarine and therefore should never be collected for food. It is most likely to be confused with the edible fried chicken mushroom, so check carefully any mushrooms that grow on the ground in clusters.

Crowded white clitocybe   *Clitocybe dilatata*

ORANGE FUNNEL-CAP (Edible with caution)
Clitocybe inversa (white spores)

Color and Description

Cap: orange-buff, pale orange-tan to orange-cinnamon to tan, smooth, center depressed and margin wavy when mature, 3–5 inches wide; flesh same color but paler than the surface, rather thin, with faint but rather sharp odor.

Gills: whitish to pale buff or pale orange-buff, running down the stem, narrow, crowded together, thin.

Stem: about the same color as the cap, usually as long as the width of the cap, or shorter, smooth or dulled by pale fibrils.

When and Where Found. Fall, on the ground, usually in rather open conifer woods.

Remarks. One of the Pacific Northwest's common clitocybes, often forming fairy rings or arcs of a circle in open places in the woods. European mushroom books say it is edible, but it should be tried very cautiously, if at all.

Orange funnel-cap   *Clitocybe inversa*

GRAYCAP (Edible but not recommended)
Clitocybe nebularis (whitish to pale yellow spores)

Color and Description
Cap: rather pale brownish gray, rounded becoming flat or slightly convex with rounded margin when mature, dry, usually with a thin, powdery bloom, 5–6 inches wide; flesh white, thick, with faint but unmistakable odor of skunk cabbage.

Gills: pale cream color, thin, close together.

Stem: colored like the gills, or flushed with the color of the cap, stout, smooth, sometimes swollen at the base.

When and Where Found. Fall, rarely in spring, on the ground in all kinds of woods.

Remarks. Edible, but it does not agree with everyone, and it tastes the way it smells. It sometimes forms very large fairy rings in woods that are open enough to allow its uninterrupted growth.

Graycap *Clitocybe nebularis*

ANISE-SCENTED CLITOCYBE (Edible)
Clitocybe odora var. *pacifica* (pinkish buff spores)

Color and Description

Cap: blue-green to pale blue-gray, at times becoming whitish with some brownish tints in the center, smooth, first rounded then irregularly upturned, 2–3 inches wide; flesh greenish white, thin, strongly scented with anise.

Gills: bluish green, touching the stem.

Stem: bluish green, 2–3 inches long.

When and Where Found. Late summer through fall, in fir needles or on edge of woods.

Remarks. The strong odor and bluish green color, which persists or intensifies in age on the gills, make it easily recognizable. Although too aromatic to be cooked alone, it may be combined with more bland mushrooms.

CLUSTERED COLLYBIA (Edible with caution)
Collybia acervata (white spores)

Color and Description

Cap: pale to dark reddish brown, fading upon losing moisture, .5–2 inches wide; rounded or flattened, smooth, moist when wet but not viscid, flesh white or flushed with reddish brown, thin, no special odor or taste.

Gills: white to pale reddish brown, rounded at the stem and barely touching it, thin, close together, narrow.

Stem: dark reddish brown, very long and slender, hollow, pliable, dry and shining above, but covered with white mycelium below.

When and Where Found. Throughout the fall season; grows in dense clusters of dozens of individuals, on rotting wood, or occasionally on the ground from buried wood. Generally considered edible; some individuals have suffered gastrointestinal upset after eating it.

Remarks. Easy to recognize because of the densely clustered growth. Discard the stems, which are tough and stringy even when cooked.

Anise-scented clitocybe   *Clitocybe odora* var. *pacifica*

Clustered collybia   *Collybia acervata*

OAK-LOVING COLLYBIA (Edible with caution)
Collybia dryophila (white spores)

Color and Description

Cap: reddish brown, tan, yellowish brown, or yellowish honey color, smooth, moist but not viscid when wet, drying silky, 2–3 inches wide; flesh white, thin, with pleasant odor and mild taste.

Gills: white or pale yellow, touching the stem slightly, usually rounded before touching, thin, crowded together.

Stem: about the same color as the cap or paler, smooth, polished, sometimes swollen and covered with matted white mycelium at the base, about as long as the width of the cap.

When and Where Found. Most abundant in fall, but may appear in spring or summer if there is enough moisture; on the ground, under alder or maple, in conifer woods, or woods of mixed conifers and hardwoods.

Remarks. Edible for most individuals but occasionally causing gastrointestinal upset. It is one of the best tasting of the Pacific Northwest's wild mushrooms. Discard the stems, which are rather tough. The very similar-looking buttery collybia *(Collybia butyracea)* has a pale pinkish buff spore print, but is otherwise hard to distinguish from *C. dryophila*. It grows in the same localities, is also edible, and is equally tasty.

Oak-loving collybia   *Collybia dryophila*

The pure cystoderma   *Cystoderma amianthinum*

THE PURE CYSTODERMA (Edibility unknown)
Cystoderma amianthinum (white spores)

Color and Description

Cap: yellow-brown to yellow-orange, paler toward the edge, cone-shaped to convex, often with a raised knob in the center, edge fringed with toothlike pieces of veil tissue, covered with fine powdery granules which disappear in age, finely to deeply wrinkled, 1–2 inches wide; flesh white, odor often of freshly husked green corn.

Gills: white to buff, attached, crowded together.

Stem: whitish and smooth above ring, yellow-buff or similar to cap color and granular below ring, 1.5–3 inches long, about .25 inch thick, ring ragged, poorly formed.

When and Where Found. Single or in groups, widespread and common; under conifers, in needles or humus, frequently in moss.

Remarks. *Cystoderma amianthinum* and other species, such as *Cystoderma fallax*, are common in the Pacific Northwest. They are not collected for food, mainly because of their small size. None are known to be poisonous, but the edibility of the different species has not really been tested. Some manuals report *Cystoderma amianthinum* as edible but mediocre. A common form of this species has an extremely strong odor of green corn, and a very wrinkled cap surface.

VELVET-STEMMED FLAMMULINA (Edible)
Flammulina velutipes (white spores)

Color and Description
Cap: yellowish to mahogany-brown, first rounded then slightly upturned, viscid, 1–2 inches wide; flesh white or yellowish, pleasant odor and flavor.

Gills: yellowish, touching the stem, unequal in length.

Stem: first yellowish, then covered with velvety dark brown hairs, 1–3 inches long.

When and Where Found. Fall, continuing into winter, although it has been found in every month of the year; on decaying wood in dense clusters.

Remarks. The velvet-stemmed flammulina is widespread in the Puget Sound area. It is a pleasant-tasting tidbit when other mushrooms have disappeared. It is easily recognized by its velvety stem.

FALSE CHANTERELLE (Edible with caution)
Hygrophoropsis aurantiaca (white spores)

Color and Description
Cap: most often orange, sometimes brown, occasionally pale cream color, rounded at first then flat to shallowly depressed, dry, suedelike, 2–4 inches wide; flesh same color as cap, thin, cottony.

Gills: orange or cream or rarely nearly white, running down the stem, narrow, close together, repeatedly forked.

Stem: colored like the cap, or paler, short, dry, dull, velvety.

Velvet-stemmed flammulina   *Flammulina velutipes*

False chanterelle   *Hygrophoropsis aurantiaca*

When and Where Found. Fall, on the ground in conifer woods or mixed conifers and hardwoods, also on rotten logs.

Remarks. Edible, but rather indigestible and scarcely to be recommended. It was formerly thought to be poisonous. The variation in color of this mushroom is truly astonishing. The orange form is the commonest, but dark brown forms with cream-colored gills and pale cream forms with nearly white gills are frequently found. The repeatedly forked gills are a constant feature and are the reason why the fungus was first described as a *Cantharellus*.

ALMOND WAXY CAP (Edible)
Hygrophorus agathosmus (white spores)

Color and Description
Cap: gray or brownish gray, flat or slightly rounded when mature, slimy when wet, 2–3 inches wide; flesh white, thick, soft, with strong, agreeable almond odor.

Gills: white, touching the stem, sometimes running slightly down it, thick, well spaced.

Stem: white, with a few granular dots at the top, stout, dry, about as long as the width of the cap.

When and Where Found. Fall, on the ground in rather dense conifer woods.

Remarks. Easily recognized by the gray slimy cap and strong almond odor. Edible, but rather tasteless; the odor disappears in cooking.

MT. BAKER WAXY CAP (Edible)
Hygrophorus bakerensis (white spores)

Color and Description
Cap: yellow-brown or rusty brown in the center, shading to almost white on the margin, rounded or flat, slimy when wet, 3–6 inches wide; flesh white, thick, with strong almond odor.

Gills: white, sometimes becoming pale cream color, running down the stem, close together or well spaced, rather thick and waxy in appearance.

Stem: white, with a few white dots at the top, stout, dry.

When and Where Found. Throughout the fall season, in conifer woods.

Almond waxy cap   *Hygrophorus agathosmus*

Mt. Baker waxy cap   *Hygrophorus bakerensis*

Remarks. In any normal mushroom season this is one of the commonest large mushrooms of the Pacific Northwest's conifer forests. It is easily recognized by the slimy, rusty brown cap with pale margin and the strong almond odor. It is edible, but opinions on its desirability differ widely.

Sooty brown waxy cap   *Hygrophorus camarophyllus*

SOOTY BROWN WAXY CAP (Edible)
Hygrophorus camarophyllus (white spores)

Color and Description

Cap: dark sooty brown or dark brown with slight olive tinge, rounded becoming flat, slightly viscid when wet, but soon becoming dry, about 2–4 inches wide; flesh white, thick, fragile, without special odor.

Gills: white or pale cream color, often tinged with gray in age, running down the stem, thick, well spaced, conspicuously interconnected with veins.

Stem: flushed with the gray-brown color of the cap, but paler, sometimes streaked or spotted with gray-brown fibrils, stout, dry, a little longer than the width of the cap.

When and Where Found. Fall, on the ground under conifers. Sometimes very abundant.

Remarks. Edible but rather tasteless, like many species of *Hygrophorus*. A very attractive related species, *H. calophyllus,* has the same color of cap and stem, but has shell-pink or pale salmon-pink gills.

CONE-SHAPED WAXY CAP (Possibly poisonous)
Hygrophorus (Hygrocybe) conicus (white spores)

Color and Description

Cap: red, orange, or yellow, cone-shaped, occasionally spreading, viscid, edge of cap uneven, often lobed, 2–4 inches wide, turning black when handled or bruised; flesh same color as the surface of the cap, thin, watery.

Gills: yellowish or olive, blackening when bruised.

Stem: orange or reddish, fragile, hollow, blackening when bruised, 2–4 inches long.

When and Where Found. Summer and fall, on the ground in Douglas fir forests, or in fields and brushy places.

Remarks. This mushroom is too small to be of much interest to the gatherer. Its widespread reputation as a poisonous species may not be entirely deserved, but there is no reason to tempt fate when so many good mushrooms of proven edibility are available.

Cone-shaped waxy cap   *Hygrophorus (Hygrocybe) conicus*

SLIMY WAXY CAP (Edible)
Hygrophorus gliocyclus (white spores)

Color and Description

Cap: white or pale cream, often more yellowish in the center, rounded then flat or shallowly concave, smooth, slimy-viscid, 2–6 inches wide or more; flesh white, thick, firm, odorless.

Gills: white, running down the stem or only fastened to it and not running down, thick, well spaced, waxy-looking.

Stem: short and thick, tapered at the base, sheathed below by the slimy universal veil which forms a glutinous ring at its upper end, satiny and white above the ring, dingy white or dingy cream color below.

When and Where Found. Fall and sometimes spring, on the ground under ponderosa pine at low elevations on the eastern slopes of the Cascade Mountains.

Remarks. An edible species, apparently relished by some people, but very disagreeable to handle because of the thick slimy veil. The slime must, of course, be removed before cooking. It is not uncommon in the locality mentioned above, but seems to be rare west of the Cascade summit.

SCARLET WAXY CAP (Edible)
Hygrophorus (Hygrocybe) miniatus (white spores)

Color and Description

Cap: brilliant scarlet when wet, fading through orange to yellow as it dries, rounded or flat, moist when wet but not viscid, about .5 to 1 inch wide; flesh red when moist, orange or yellow on losing moisture, thin, fragile, odorless.

Gills: usually yellow but may be orange or red, waxy in appearance, touching the stem, often notched.

Stem: scarlet when moist, fading like the cap to orange then yellow, smooth, almost translucent, varying in length from the width of the cap to several times its width.

When and Where Found. Fall, on the ground in woods, usually under conifers.

Slimy waxy cap   *Hygrophorus gliocyclus*

Scarlet waxy cap   *Hygrophorus (Hygrocybe) miniatus*

Remarks. This is a beautiful little mushroom, showing an astonishing change in color as it dries out. It is especially attractive when growing in a bed of moss, as it often does. It is edible, but much too small to be of any importance for the table.

Blushing hygrophorus   *Hygrophorus pudorinus*

BLUSHING HYGROPHORUS (Edible)
Hygrophorus pudorinus (white spores)

Color and Description

Cap: pale tan to pinkish or pinkish buff, rounded to flattened, edge enrolled and minutely white downy, smooth, viscid, 2–5 inches wide; flesh white or tinged pink; at times slightly fragrant.

Gills: white to pallid or pale pinkish, running slightly down the stem, narrow, slightly spaced, thickish, sometimes forked.

Stem: white to buff or pinkish, upper portion covered with fine scale-like points that become reddish in age, 2–4 inches long, often fairly thick, surface dry or slightly sticky; no veil.

When and Where Found. Late summer and fall seasons, scattered or in groups, typically under conifers. Widespread, at times abundant in some areas.

Remarks. This beautiful *Hygrophorus* comes in various color forms with some specimens being white or gray rather than tan to pinkish. It is generally rated as a good edible, but bitter taste may make some forms inedible or of poor quality. A weak solution of potassium hydroxide, when applied to the stem apex, gives a strong orange reaction characteristic of the species.

LARCH WAXY CAP (Edible)
Hygrophorus speciosus (white spores)

Color and Description

Cap: orange to orange-red, fading to yellow in age, rounded to flattened, sometimes with a knoblike center, slimy-sticky, 1–2 inches wide; flesh white to yellowish, mild odor and taste.

Gills: white to yellowish, often with yellowish edges, thick, waxy-looking, well spaced, running down the stem, but sometimes not strongly so.

Stem: 2–4 inches long, white to yellow or orange, coated by a slimy gluten which as it dries stains the stem orange.

When and Where Found. Fruits in the late summer and fall on the ground in conifer forests or bogs containing larch. At times common.

Remarks. The larch waxy cap is common in the western mountains and is edible but apparently not of high quality. *Hygrophorus hypothejus*, a similar-looking species, is widespread and grows in

Larch waxy cap   *Hygrophorus speciosus*

association with a variety of conifers, particularly two-needle pines. Typically it has a brown, olive or olive-brown color to the fresh caps but may be yellow, orange, or reddish in age. The slimy lower stem may be olive-brown, yellowish, orange, or scarlet. It also is edible.

SUBALPINE WAXY CAP (Edible)
Hygrophorus subalpinus (white spores)

Color and Description

Cap: pure white, rounded or flat, smooth, viscid when wet but soon drying and becoming shining, 2–4 inches wide or more; flesh white, thick, firm, odorless.

Gills: white, often tinged with cream in older caps, running down the stem, rather narrow.

Stem: shorter than the width of the cap, very thick, with a large bulb having a flat upper edge, to which is attached a flaring, narrow, fibrous ring, white and silky above, the bulb white but with adhering soil particles.

When and Where Found. Spring and early summer, and sometimes again in the fall; on the ground under conifers, usually at high elevations in the Cascade Mountains, often not far from melting snow.

Remarks. This massive, handsome, pure white mushroom is easily recognized by its bulbous stem with a narrow, flaring ring—an unusual feature for a *Hygrophorus*. To the beginner it might appear to have a volva and thus seem to be an amanita, but none of the amanitas have gills that run down the stem. It also looks something like *Russula brevipes*, but does not have that species' chalklike flesh, and has a viscid cap. It is edible, but has very little flavor.

WESTERN PURPLE LACCARIA (Edible)
Laccaria amethysteo-occidentalis (white spores)

Color and Description

Cap: violet-purple when moist, lighter when dry, rounded then expanded, margin irregular, 1–3 inches wide; flesh lavender, thin, dry.

Gills: purple, broad, irregular, touching stem.

Subalpine waxy cap   *Hygrophorus subalpinus*

Western purple laccaria   *Laccaria amethysteo-occidentalis*

Stem: purple, shaded violet at base, tough, strongly striate, often curved, single or in clusters, 3–4 inches long.

When and Where Found. Early to late fall, in Douglas fir forests, or on the edge of woodlands, often in bracken fern.

Remarks. Edible, but of poor quality. Its color makes it unmistakable and its beauty is its justification for existence. Its only rival is the violet cortinarius, which has brown spores and a cobwebby veil. *Laccaria bicolor,* a mushroom with a pinkish flesh-colored cap, at times with an admixture of brown or orange, vinaceous to pinkish gills, and a stem concolorous with the cap, except for the violet base, is another common western species similar in size to the western purple laccaria.

COMMON LACCARIA (Edible)
Laccaria laccata (white spores)

Color and Description
Cap: orange-brown when fresh, becoming buff, moist to dry, first rounded then expanded, often hollow in the center and irregularly ruffled on the margin, mostly .5–2 inches wide; flesh some shade of surface color, thin.

Gills: pinkish to dull rose, broad, irregular, touching stem.

Stem: same color as cap surface, shaded whitish at the base, fibrous, scurfy, 1–4 inches long.

When and Where Found. Late summer to late fall, occasionally in spring; growing alone, scattered, or several together, rarely in clusters; in the forest, sometimes along old roads.

Remarks. A mushroom seen often in many situations, edible but rather tough and tasteless. May be easily distinguished from similarly colored species of *Lactarius* because it has no milky juice.

Common laccaria   *Laccaria laccata*

Delicious milky cap   *Lactarius deliciosus*

DELICIOUS MILKY CAP (Edible)
Lactarius deliciosus (yellowish spores)

Color and Description

Cap: orange, zoned with darker orange, often staining green with age, first rounded then upturned and depressed in center, margin inrolled, usually 2–4 inches wide; flesh deep yellow, taste mild, exuding orange milk when cut.

Gills: orange, regular, running down the stem, exuding orange milk when cut, often staining green.

Stem: orange, short, stout, 2–4 inches long.

When and Where Found. Late summer through fall, on the ground in forested areas, often in old second-growth Douglas fir forests or under or near Sitka spruce near the Pacific Ocean.

Remarks. Occasionally in favorable seasons a giant form of this mushroom is found, 4–14 inches across. It is identical in all characteristics with the usual form. The delicious milky cap has been eaten for many hundreds of years. There is a picture of it in a mural in the ruins of Herculaneum.

ORANGE MILKY CAP (Edible)
Lactarius luculentus (white to pale ivory spores)

Color and Description

Cap: bright red to red-orange at center, orange on the margin, rounded then flat or slightly depressed and usually with a small knob in the center, smooth, viscid when wet, 1–3 inches wide; flesh orange-buff, thin, brittle, with mild or slightly bitter or astringent taste but not peppery, where cut exuding abundant white milk that does not change color.

Gills: orange-buff, or yellow tinged with orange, touching the stem, sometimes running down it, thin, close together, exuding copious white milk where cut.

Stem: shaded with orange colors of the cap, slender, soon hollow, moist but not viscid.

When and Where Found. Throughout the fall season, on the ground in conifer forests or in mixed woods.

Remarks. Edible, but of poor quality; the bitter taste often persists after the specimens have been cooked. The viscid red to orange cap, orange-buff gills, and white, mild milk distinguish it. This species is one of several of the orange milky caps previously grouped under the name *Lactarius aurantiacus.*

Orange milky cap   *Lactarius luculentus*

Pale-capped violet-latex lactarius   *Lactarius pallescens* var. *pallescens*

PALE-CAPPED VIOLET-LATEX LACTARIUS (Poisonous)
Lactarius pallescens var. *pallescens* (white to creamy spores)

Color and Description

Cap: milk white at first, becoming grayish to grayish brown or light brown or slightly lavender, in age with orange yellow stains, slimy to sticky, broadly rounded to somewhat depressed centrally, edge incurved to decurved, 1.5–4 inches wide; flesh white, exuding copious white milk when cut which stains tissue lilac then lilac-brown.

Gills: white, staining lilac, with orange-yellow stains along edges in age, squarely attached or slightly running down the stem, close together to somewhat spaced.

Stem: white, color changing like the cap, 1–5 inches long, fairly thick, slimy to sticky then shiny when dry.

When and Where Found. Fruits in the late summer and fall seasons. On the ground in soil, humus or moss, in conifer or mixed forests; solitary, scattered or in small groups.

Remarks. This is a common and widespread coastal and montane species in the Pacific Northwest. It often occurs in second growth hemlock stands in the Puget Sound region. *Lactarius pallescens* var. *pallescens* is a close relative of *L. uvidus,* this group being characterized by purple staining latex or flesh. All are believed to be poisonous and should be avoided as food.

Slimy milky cap   *Lactarius pseudomucidus*

SLIMY MILKY CAP (Inedible)
Lactarius pseudomucidus (white spores)

Color and Description

Cap: slate gray or brownish gray, sometimes pale on the margin, flat or shallowly depressed in the center, smooth, slimy when wet, about 2 inches wide; flesh white or tinged gray, thin, exuding white milk where broken, peppery taste.

Gills: white, exuding white milk where cut, turning pale gray-green where the milk dries, touching the stem or running slightly down it, thin, close together.

Stem: same color as the cap, slender, soon hollow, smooth, viscid.

When and Where Found. Fall, on the ground under conifers.

Remarks. Edibility unknown, but should be avoided, since peppery *Lactarii* are not safe for experimentation. This is one of the Pacific Northwest's commonest species of *Lactarius*, easily recognized by its slimy gray cap and stem, contrasting nicely with the white gills. The milk itself does not change color when exposed to air, but becomes pale gray-green where it dries in contact with the flesh or gills. This lactarius has previously been called *Lactarius mucidus*.

Woolly milky cap   *Lactarius pubescens* var. *betulae*

WOOLLY MILKY CAP (Inedible)
Lactarius pubescens var. *betulae* (white to cream spores)

Color and Description
Cap: creamy white to pale pinkish or pale cinnamon-pink, usually the center slightly darker or more cinnamon, first rounded then spreading, depressed in center, margin inrolled with downy edge, 3–4 inches wide; flesh white or pinkish, exuding a scanty white milk which becomes yellowish and stains the flesh, with a peppery taste that grows very strong with chewing.

Gills: pinkish, close together, narrow, touching the stem or running down it.

Stem: whitish or pinkish, short, stout, 2–3 inches long.

When and Where Found. Usually most abundant in the fall, also appearing in spring or summer if enough moisture is available; associated with birch trees.

Remarks. This is one of several woolly milky caps. The various species, which include *Lactarius torminosus,* are difficult to identify. Generally they are regarded as poisonous, though their peppery flavor is destroyed by cooking them long enough, and they are eaten in some parts of Europe. There seems little point in taking the risk of eating them, however, with plenty of good mushrooms available. Certain of the woolly milky caps occur in lawns or parking strips where white or paper birch trees have been planted. They have become well established with these plantings in western Washington and British Columbia.

Red-juice milky cap \ *Lactarius rubrilacteus*

RED-JUICE MILKY CAP (Edible)
Lactarius rubrilacteus (pale yellowish spores)

Color and Description

Cap: rich carrot color to sordid orange or reddish brown, often with alternating zones of darker and lighter colors, duller in age and usually with greenish stains or flushes; smooth, first rounded then depressed in the center, margin inrolled, slightly viscid, 2–4 inches wide; flesh yellowish white, stained greenish in age, exuding a dark red, milky fluid when broken, with mild taste.

Gills: pinkish cinnamon to reddish or dull purplish red, regular, running down the stem, exuding dark red milk when cut or broken, often becoming stained with green.

Stem: color similar to but usually darker than the cap, short, stout, older specimens mottled with green, 2–4 inches long.

When and Where Found. Early to late fall, often abundant on the ground in fir needles in young second-growth Douglas fir forests.

Remarks. Similar to the delicious milky cap, but having red milk instead of orange. Although less well known than the delicious milky cap, it has a better flavor and more substance. A name earlier used for this species was *Lactarius sanguifluus*.

RED MILKY CAP (Poisonous)
Lactarius rufus (white spores)

Color and Description

Cap: dull red or brownish red or brick red, flat or slightly rounded often with a small, sharp knob in the center, smooth, not viscid, 2–3 inches wide; flesh white tinged with pink, exuding a white milk where cut, taste slowly becoming intolerably peppery.

Gills: pallid at first, then becoming more and more flushed with the reddish color of the cap, exuding white milk where broken or cut, touching the stem, thin, close together.

Stem: same color as the cap, dry, smooth, usually longer than the width of the cap.

When and Where Found. Throughout the fall, in conifer forests, often in swampy places.

Remarks. Poisonous. A small piece of the mushroom seems to have a mild taste at first, but after about a minute of chewing the burning sensation begins, gradually becoming more and more intense and lasting a long time. Few mushrooms are as peppery as this one.

Red milky cap   *Lactarius rufus*

PITTED MILKY CAP (Considered poisonous)
Lactarius scrobiculatus var. *canadensis* (white to very pale cream spores)

Color and Description

Cap: yellow, often with concentric zones of paler and darker yellow, broadly depressed in the center, margin at first inrolled and hairy, finally flat and smooth, viscid, about 3–6 inches wide; flesh thick, firm, pallid, exuding white milk that quickly turns sulphur yellow in contact with the air, very peppery taste.

Gills: pale yellow, where broken exuding white milk that turns yellow, touching the stem or sometimes running slightly down it, thin, rather narrow.

Stem: paler yellow than the cap, with small, shallow, round or oval sunken spots that often are of a brighter color than the surface, short and stout, hollow, moist but not viscid.

When and Where Found. Fall, on the ground in conifer woods.

Remarks. To be avoided; considered by many to be poisonous. This is a common lactarius in the Pacific Northwest, easily recognized by the yellow colors and the white, peppery milk that quickly turns yellow upon exposure to air. It is often abundant in older conifer forests, especially in the mountains.

Pitted milky cap *Lactarius scrobiculatus* var. *canadensis*

Shaggy-stalked lepiota   *Lepiota clypeolaria*

SHAGGY-STALKED LEPIOTA (Considered poisonous)
Lepiota clypeolaria (white spores)

Color and Description

Cap: brownish to crust brown at the center, yellowish brown to yellowish on the margin, scaly on the margin and smooth at very center, dry, bell- to cone-shaped then rounded to somewhat flattened with a distinct central knob, 1–3 inches wide; flesh white.

Gills: white, free, first covered by a whitish veil that leaves a poorly formed ragged ring of fibrils near the stem apex and patches of ragged tissue on the cap edge.

Stem: whitish above the ring, covered with dense, yellow-brown woolly scales or ragged patches from the ring downward, 2–4 inches long, a quarter inch thick, not much enlarged at the base.

When and Where Found. Late summer and fall in the Pacific Northwest, into the winter season further south along the Pacific Coast; on the ground in coniferous or mixed wood, widespread and fairly common.

Remarks. The Pacific Northwest has a variety of small- to medium-sized species of *Lepiota*. Identification of species is difficult and certain ones, such as *Lepiota clypeolaria* and *L. rubrotincta,* are reported as poisonous, the latter causing gastrointestinal upset. In addition, some species, such as *Lepiota helveola,* are known to be deadly. Avoid all of them.

DEADLY LEPIOTA (Deadly poisonous)
Lepiota helveola (white spores)

Color and Description

Cap: pinkish brown to more reddish brown in age or when bruised, center smooth or velvety, margin breaking into concentric scales exposing a pale whitish yellow to pinkish ground color, edge more or less fringed, rounded to flattened with a slight knob, dry, 1–2 inches wide; flesh white, thick at the center; odor musty.

Gills: white to creamy yellow, free or slightly attached to the stem, close together.

Stem: whitish to pinkish, coated below the slight ring with small scales colored like the cap, 1–2 inches long, fragile; veil present in young specimens.

When and Where Found. Fall and winter seasons on the Pacific Coast depending on weather and location. On the ground under oaks or in mixed woods.

Remarks. There are apparently several small lepiotas that are similar in appearance to *Lepiota helveola,* for example, *L. subincarnata.* All should be considered extremely dangerous since they contain the deadly amatoxins. There are at least two cases of poisoning from this group of lepiotas on the west coast. Do not eat small- to medium-sized lepiotas.

Deadly lepiota   *Lepiota helveola*

Woods blewits *Lepista nuda*

WOODS BLEWITS (Edible)
Lepista nuda (pinkish buff spores)

Color and Description

Cap: purple masked with brown, eventually fading to tan or pallid, first rounded then with margin upturned irregularly, 3–5 inches wide; flesh dull purple or grayish, pleasant odor.

Gills: lavender, notched before touching stem.

Stem: lavender, stout, larger at base, 3–4 inches long, sometimes clustered.

When and Where Found. Fall until after frost, or in winter and spring in milder regions; in leaves in deciduous woods or in needles under Douglas firs and other conifers, sometimes in thick grass at the edge of woods, often in compost heaps or in sawdust.

Remarks. The common name, blewits (blue hats), comes from England, where it is thought the mature cap looks like a jaunty cocked blue hat. This mushroom has long been a favorite among the edible species. The flavor is delicate but very pleasant. Several names have been used for it, the commonest ones being *Tricholoma nuda* and *T. personatum;* more recently, some authors have called it *Clitocybe nuda.*

WHITE LEPIOTA (Edible with caution)
Leucoagaricus (Lepiota) naucinus (white spores)

Color and Description
Cap: white, occasionally tinged with gray, smooth like kidskin, first rounded then flat, 3–10 inches wide; flesh white, unchanging.

Gills: white, usually becoming dull pink with age, first covered with a white veil which, on breaking, becomes a movable ring on the stem.

Stem: white, slender, larger at the base; *no cup*.

When and Where Found. Late summer and fall, on the ground in parking strips, open meadows, lawns, occasionally in plowed fields, always in the open.

Remarks. As this mushroom greatly resembles some forms of the poisonous amanitas, care should be taken in gathering it. Pick the entire stem, to be sure there is no volva or cup at the base. The cap and stem of the white lepiota may develop yellow stains when handled and in some forms the spore deposit will be pinkish rather than white. One form of this lepiota has a gray cap, sometimes densely covered with minute, branlike gray scales, but in all other ways resembles the normal white form. This gray form is reported to cause stomach upset in some persons, whereas others eat it with no ill effects. It and the regular white form should, of course, be tried cautiously the first time.

White lepiota   *Leucoagaricus (Lepiota) naucinus*

White false paxillus   *Leucopaxillus albissimus*

WHITE FALSE PAXILLUS (Inedible)
Leucopaxillus albissimus (white spores)

Color and Description

Cap: white to pale cream, rounded, dry, dull, suedelike, 2–4 inches wide; flesh white, thick, rather tough, mild or bitter taste.

Gills: White, usually running down the stem, but sometimes merely fastened to it and not running down, thin, close together.

Stem: white or cream, with a mat of white mycelium binding a lump of needles or other forest litter to the base, rather short and stout.

When and Where Found. Fall, on the ground under conifers or hardwoods.

Remarks. Can be eaten, but is not recommended. There are two varieties: var. *albissimus* is bitter and hence inedible; var. *lentus* has a mild taste but is rather tough and indigestible.

BITTER FALSE PAXILLUS (Inedible)
Leucopaxillus amarus (white spores)

Color and Description

Cap: reddish cinnamon color to cinnamon, usually paler on the margin, rounded, dry, suedelike, about 3–5 inches wide; flesh white, thick, bitter taste.

Gills: white or pale cream, usually notched at the stem, occasionally running down it somewhat, thin, close together.

Bitter false paxillus   *Leucopaxillus amarus*

Stem: white, short and thick, dry, dull, often with a clublike swollen base, and often with abundant mycelium binding the needles or leaves together at the base.

When and Where Found. Fall, on the ground under conifers or hardwoods. Often very abundant.

Remarks. Inedible because of the bitter taste which no amount of cooking will remove. This and the white false paxillus sometimes form large fairy rings in open places in the forest.

FRIED CHICKEN MUSHROOM (Edible)
Lyophyllum decastes (white spores)

Color and Description
Cap: cream-white or tan, smooth, persistently rounded, sometimes irregular on the margin, 3–5 inches wide; flesh white, firm.

Gills: white, touching or running slightly down the stem.

Stem: cream-white, curved from the pressure of the densely clustered caps, sometimes large numbers in one cluster.

When and Where Found. Late fall after heavy rains, occasionally in the spring; in heavy clay soil on margins of roads, often half hidden in heavy grass or leaves.

Remarks. The curious soapy feel of the pale brown or tan caps, together with the cluster, are helpful in distinguishing the fried chicken mushroom. Edible and of good flavor, as the common name indicates; considered by many to be one of the best of the Pacific Northwest's edible mushrooms. Because there are poisonous mushrooms that are similar in appearance, you should observe the following precautions when gathering the fried chicken mushroom: (1) Be sure that your specimens are growing in clusters of four or five or more; discard solitary specimens, even if you think they are all right. (2) Be sure that the spore print is white and not pink as in the poisonous species of *Entoloma*. Better yet, in case of doubt, look at the spores with a microscope. The spores of an *Entoloma* are angular in outline, those of a *Lyophyllum* are even. *Clitocybe dilatata,* a mushroom often occurring in the same habitat as the fried chicken mushroom, and also growing in clusters, is reported to contain the poison muscarine. It also has white spores; the caps are grayish at first, as are the stems, become whitish in age, and are chalky white in drier weather. Therefore usually the fruit bodies are paler or whiter in color than the fried chicken mushroom.

Fried chicken mushroom   *Lyophyllum decastes*

SHAGGY LEPIOTA (Edible with caution)
Macrolepiota (Lepiota) rachodes (white spores)

Color and Description

Cap: tan or fawn color in young specimens, but as the cap expands the surface breaks into pointed scales, giving the rough and shaggy appearance, first rounded then flattened, 3–10 inches wide; flesh white, then grayish, turning orangish to pinkish to red when broken or bruised.

Gills: white, soft, free from the stem, first covered with a thick veil.

Stem: white, much larger at the base, having a large, thick ring, the remains of the veil.

When and Where Found. Fall or occasionally in the spring or summer, in the open near outbuildings, on compost, on lawns, in meadows, along roadsides.

Remarks. *M. rachodes* is one of the best edible mushrooms, easily recognized by its coarse scaly cap, large thick ring, large bulb at the base of the stem, and orange to red staining of its flesh and gills where bruised. Eat it with caution, however, since some individuals develop gastric upset from eating it. The shaggy lepiota is quite similar in appearance to the poisonous, green-spored *Chlorophyllum molybdites;* in fact, it is very difficult to tell the difference between the buttons of the two species. The green-spored lepiota, however, has not so far been

Shaggy lepiota   *Macrolepiota (Lepiota) rachodes*

Fairy ring mushroom   *Marasmius oreades*

reported north of central California on the Pacific Coast, so there would seem to be little danger of being poisoned by it in northern California or the Pacific Northwest.

FAIRY RING MUSHROOM (Edible)
Marasmius oreades (white spores)

Color and Description

Cap: cream-white, buff, or tan to reddish tan, first rounded, then flat and irregular on margin, 1–2 inches wide; flesh white, thin, nutty flavor.

Gills: cream-white, almost free to free from the stem, broad, well spaced, long and short intermixed.

Stem: cream-white or tinted with cap colors, tough, rough with minute hairs on the lower portion, 2–3 inches long.

When and Where Found. Spring, summer, and fall after rains, in grass lawns, parking strips, golf courses, or meadows, always in the open, often forming fairy rings.

Remarks: Widespread, this mushroom is considered a pest by home-owners, but it has a good flavor and is easily dried. The tough stems should be discarded. Occasionally the sweat-producing clitocybe also grows in partial circles on lawns, but it is easily recognized by the whitish to pale buff gills that run down the stem.

Garlic marasmius   *Marasmius scorodonius*

GARLIC MARASMIUS (Edible)
Marasmius scorodonius (white spores)

Color and Description
Cap: tan or brownish, .25–1.25 inches wide; flesh thin, with strong garlic taste and odor.

Gills: cream-white, narrow.

Stems: brown, short, tough, polished, 1–2.5 inches long.

When and Where Found. Fall, on twigs and debris, commonly on dead fern stems or fir needles in Douglas fir forests. Sometimes found by the odor.

Remarks. A small mushroom, but with a strong garlic taste and odor, so much so that a cap or two will flavor other tasteless mushrooms.

CHANGEABLE MELANOLEUCA (Edible with caution)
Melanoleuca melaleuca (white spores)

Color and Description
Cap: smoky brown to dark brown, fading somewhat in age, smooth, moist to dry, rounded to flatten with a small, low knob, 1–3 inches wide; flesh thin, whitish.

Changeable melanoleuca   *Melanoleuca melaleuca*

Gills: white, attached but deeply notched at the stem.

Stem: white with brownish or dark hairs running lengthwise, 1–3 inches long, with the base equal or slightly swollen.

When and Where Found. Fruits in the summer and fall or into the winter further south on the Pacific Coast. Solitary to scattered, widespread, in pastures, other open areas, and in open woods.

Remarks. There are several melanoleucas in the Pacific Northwest but the species are not easily identified. Many are reported as edible, some as inedible, and several are unknown. They should be eaten with caution if at all. The genus *Melanoleuca* has a characteristic appearance. The cap is wide in relation to the tall, narrow stem, has a smooth surface and a knob in the center. There is no veil and the stem often is easily broken.

THE CLEAN MYCENA (Not recommended)
Mycena pura (white spores)

Color and Description
Cap: variously colored, rose red, purplish, lilac-gray or yellowish white with purplish tents at the center, cone-shaped to rounded or flattened with a broad, low knob at the center, moist, radially lined,

1–2 inches wide; flesh moderately thin, purplish to whitish, odor and taste distinctly radish-like.

Gills: whitish, grayish to purplish or with pinkish tones, edges whitish, attached to the stem, broad, veined between.

Stem: white to pink or purplish tinged, smooth or with twisted lines, 1–4 inches long, up to .25 inch thick.

When and Where Found. Spring, summer, fall and winter where weather permits; widespread and often common in forested areas.

Remarks. Though large for a *Mycena,* the clean mycena is usually too small to be collected for food. It is eaten by some individuals, but it is not recommended, particularly in large quantities. It has been reported to contain traces of muscarine, a toxin that affects the sympathetic nervous system.

The clean mycena   *Mycena pura*

RED-ORANGE MYCENA (Inedible)
Mycena strobilinoides (white spores)

Color and Description

Cap: scarlet to red, at times fading to yellowish, moist to tacky, smooth, with radial lines, margin somewhat scalloped when mature, usually less than 1 inch wide, cone-shaped to bell-shaped; flesh thin.

Gills: attached to the stem, yellow to light pinkish orange with scarlet edges.

Stem: 1–2 inches long, thin, orange to orange-yellow or paler, with fine hair or smooth, the base with orange fibrils.

When and Where Found. Usually forming extensive fruitings, in "troops," on conifer needles in the late summer and fall. Common, especially in mountain forests of fir and other conifers.

Remarks. This small, attractive mushroom is of no consequence as an edible. It is one of the most common mycenas in the Pacific Northwest and like many of its kind covers the needle beds during cool, moist autumns.

Red-orange mycena   *Mycena strobilinoides*

LATE OYSTER MUSHROOM (Edible)
Panellus serotinus (white spores)

Color and Description

Cap: dull green, yellowish green, bluish gray or dull brown, or mottled with two or all of these colors, shell-shaped or fan-shaped, smooth, viscid, about 2–5 inches wide, flesh white, thick, with a gelatinous layer near the surface, odorless.

Gills: yellow, attached to the stem or "false stem" close together, thin.

Stem: usually there is a thickened cushionlike structure called a "false stem" on the margin of the cap where it is attached to the wood, it is hairy or velvety, usually yellow, sometimes flecked with brown or dull green.

When and Where Found. Late fall, sometimes continuing well into winter, growing by preference on logs or stumps of wild cherry, but also on other hardwoods.

Remarks. Edible, but not of good quality; it may develop a bitter taste when cooked. It is easily recognized by its yellow gills and sticky greenish or bluish gray cap. Its preference for cold temperatures causes it to appear in the Pacific Northwest toward the end of the mushroom season and to continue fruiting after most other mushrooms have disappeared.

ANGEL'S WINGS (Edible)
Pleurocybella (Pleurotus) porrigens (white spores)

Color and Description

Cap: pure white at first, becoming pale cream with age, fan-shaped or spatula-shaped or like a clamshell, smooth, 2–4 inches wide; flesh white, thin, firm, no special odor.

Gills: white or pallid cream, thin, close together, narrow.

Stem: absent, the cap being attached to the wood by its margin.

When and Where Found. Throughout the fall season, rarely in spring, always on conifer logs or stumps.

Remarks. Edible, and, according to some, better than the oyster mushroom. Although thin-fleshed and rather small, it often grows in such quantities that there is no difficulty getting enough for the table.

Late oyster mushroom   *Panellus serotinus*

Angel's wings   *Pleurocybella (Pleurotus) porrigens*

Oyster mushroom *Pleurotus ostreatus*

OYSTER MUSHROOM (Edible)
Pleurotus ostreatus (dull lilac spores)

Color and Description

Cap: brownish gray to oyster gray or white, attached at the side, 2–5 inches wide; flesh white, thin.

Gills: white or grayish, sometimes running together at point of attachment.

Stem: usually absent, the caps growing one above the other in series along a tree or log.

When and Where Found. Spring, late summer, and early fall, usually on stumps or logs of alder, willow, maple, or cottonwood.

Remarks. The various types of oyster mushroom, whether white or brownish to gray, are all edible and are very good when young. Several crops may be gathered in one season from the same tree or log. If the log is carried home to the yard and kept moist, sometimes the mushrooms will continue to fruit.

SHORT-STEMMED RUSSULA (Edible)
Russula brevipes (white to very pale cream spores)

Color and Description

Cap: white at first, becoming a dingy buff to dingy brown in older specimens, deeply depressed in the center, with rounded margin, dry, dull, 4–14 inches wide; flesh white, thick, firm, with very little odor and a mild to faintly peppery taste.

Gills: white at first, pale cream in age, with tendency to stain brown, running down the stem, thin, narrow, close together.

Stem: white, sometimes staining brown, dry, dull, short and thick, 2–6 inches long.

When and Where Found. Fall, occasionally in spring or summer if there is enough moisture, on the ground in conifer woods.

Remarks. Edible but rather tasteless; it is perhaps best cooked with meat or in sauces, whose flavor it then assumes. There has been much confusion about this russula in the Pacific Northwest. For years

Short-stemmed russula   *Russula brevipes*

it, its varieties, and *Russula cascadensis* have been gathered and eaten as *R. delica* by mushroom hunters of the region. However, according to the North American expert on russulas, Dr. R. L. Shaffer, the *R. delica* of Europe has thick, well-spaced gills, and spores that are differently ornamented than those of the Pacific Northwest species. The variety *acrior* of *R. brevipes* has a slight to strong peppery taste, gills tinged with bluish green, and occasionally a narrow blue-green band on the stem where the gills touch it. It too is edible, the peppery taste disappearing in cooking.

EMETIC RUSSULA (Poisonous)
Russula emetica (white spores)

Color and Description
Cap: rosy red, first rounded then flat, viscid when wet, margin furrowed, 2–4 inches wide; flesh white, firm, taste quickly and intensely peppery.
Gills: white, thin, brittle.
Stem: white, 2–3 inches long, very fragile.
When and Where Found. Late summer and fall, in Douglas fir forests, in moss or on needles.
Remarks. Considered poisonous by most authorities, though some say it is edible after thorough cooking. There seems to be little point in tempting fate by eating it, when so many safe, genuinely good edible mushrooms are available. Its distinguishing features are the bright red cap, pure white gills and stem, and intensely peppery taste (see the remarks under *Russula rosacea*). There are several closely related russulas with white stem and gills and peppery taste, but their caps are various shades of coppery pink, rosy salmon, and yellow.

ALMOND-SCENTED RUSSULA (Inedible)
Russula laurocerasi (pale orange-yellow spores)

Color and Description
Cap: pale brownish ochre to yellow-brown, usually darker towards the center, depressed in the center, 1–5 inches wide, margin conspicuously lined, slimy and shiny when fresh or moist; flesh white to

Emetic russula   *Russula emetica*

Almond-scented russula   *Russula laurocerasi*

whitish, brittle, taste unpleasant, acrid to bitterish, almond odor.

Gills: whitish to pale cream color, often brown spotted, touching the stem, fairly broad, close together to somewhat spaced, often forked.

Stem: white or whitish, sometimes buff or yellowish to brownish, 1–4 inches long, dull.

When and Where Found. Late summer and fall seasons, on the ground in conifer and broadleaf or mixed forest.

Remarks. *Russula laurocerasi,* like the fetid russula, *Russula foetens,* is inedible because of its disagreeable taste. The fetid russula is similar to the almond scented russula but is usually larger, darker, and develops a strong fetid odor.

BLACKENING RUSSULA (Edible)
Russula nigricans (white spores)

Color and Description

Cap: white at first, slowly turning dingy brown then black with age, rounded, slightly sticky to dry, dull, 3–6 or sometimes 8–10, inches wide; flesh slowly turning red then black where bruised or cut, thick, hard, no special odor, mild taste.

Gills: pale cream when young, gradually becoming gray then black in old specimens, changing color like the flesh where bruised, touching the stem, alternating long and short gills; thick, well spaced, brittle.

Stem: white or dingy pallid cream, becoming black like the cap with age, changing color like the flesh where bruised, short and very stout, dull.

When and Where Found. Throughout the fall season, on the ground in forests of conifers or conifers and hardwoods; common throughout the Pacific Northwest, especially in the mountains.

Remarks. Edible when young and free of larvae. The unprepossessing appearance of older specimens that have begun to turn black usually keeps them out of the frying pan. The change to red then black of the bruised flesh is distinctive for *Russula nigricans* and its relatives. Another russula of the Pacific Northwest, *Russula densifolia,* has this same bruising reaction, but has the gills close together

Blackening russula   *Russula nigricans*

and a brown viscid cap that dries as though varnished. Still another species, *Russula dissimulans*, also bruises red then black. It has a dry cap surface that is white at first then turns brown to black, and its gills are close together or slightly spaced. *Russula albonigra* looks very much like *R. nigricans*, but has closer gills and turns black directly when bruised, without first turning red. Both of these other species, like *R. nigricans*, are edible but of poor quality. *Russula subnigricans*, a Japanese species related to the blackening russula, is poisonous and has caused several fatalities in Japan.

WESTERN RUSSULA (Edible)
Russula occidentalis (cream spores)

Color and Description
Cap: color variable, usually light purplish with a pale yellow or olive greenish center sometimes grayish red centrally, the various

Western russula   *Russula occidentalis*

colors sometimes mixed with brown or more purplish overall, flat to
broadly rounded with the center depressed, viscid when fresh, drying
dull or somewhat shiny, slightly striate on the margin, 2–5 inches
wide; flesh white bruising reddish then gray to black, soft, odor
pleasant, mild taste.

Gills: pale yellow, edges often blackening in age, touching the
stem, close together or slightly spaced in age.

Stem: white bruising reddish then dark gray to black, soft and
spongy within, up to about 2 inches long.

When and Where Found. Late summer and into the fall season,
on the ground in conifer woods. Sometimes common in the mountains of western Washington.

Remarks. The typically purplish cap with a greenish yellow center
and the staining reaction, from reddish or salmon to blackish, are
helpful characteristics when identifying this russula. At least two
other species which turn reddish then blackish when bruised or cut are
Russula decolorans, which has a coppery orange-red cap, and *Russula
claroflava,* with a bright yellow cap.

COMB RUSSULA (Edible)
Russula pectinata (pale cream spores)

Color and Description

Cap: dark brown in the center, paler brown on the margin, flat or shallowly depressed in the center, margin conspicuously furrowed, viscid when wet, about 3 inches wide; flesh white, firm, not changing color where bruised, with peppery taste, unpleasant odor, of coal-tar gas.

Gills: white at first, then pallid cream color, touching the stem, sometimes running down it slightly.

Stem: white, sometimes with brown stains which are not from bruising, often with a little spot or two of orange-red at the very base, short, stout, dry, dull or shiny.

When and Where Found. Fall, in conifer woods, also rather frequently on lawns or in open grassy places under or near conifers.

Remarks. Although this russula is colored somewhat like *Russula foetens,* it lacks the strong, fetid odor. It is edible, but has little to recommend it; prolonged cooking destroys almost all the peppery taste.

Comb russula   *Russula pectinata*

ROSE-RED RUSSULA (Inedible)
Russula rosacea (yellow spores)

Color and Description

Cap: dries to a shining, bright red, flat or a little depressed at the center, viscid when wet, 2–4 inches wide; flesh white, thick, firm, not changing color where bruised, odorless, taste quickly very peppery.

Gills: cream color to rather pale yellow, touching the stem or running down it slightly.

Stem: rose-colored or red, stout, about as long as the width of the cap.

When and Where Found. Fall, in conifer woods or in open grassy places near conifers.

Remarks. Edibility unknown; best avoided because of the intensely peppery taste. This russula is often mistaken for *Russula emetica* because of its red cap and peppery taste, but *R. rosacea* has a rose or red stem and yellowish gills, whereas both the stem and gills of *R. emetica* are pure white. In color and general appearance it is almost exactly like the scarlet variety of *R. xerampelina,* but that species has a mild taste, stains brown where bruised, and has an odor of shrimp.

Rose-red russula   *Russula rosacea*

WOODLAND RUSSULA (Edible)
Russula xerampelina (yellow spores)

Color and Description

Cap: various shades of purple, usually very dark purple more or less flushed with brown, also red or dark brown to olive-green, first rounded, then margin upturned and center depressed, viscid when wet, 4–12 inches wide; flesh white or creamy, staining yellowish, then brown, thick, with odor of shrimp when old, upon drying, or while being cooked.

Gills: cream-white, broad, brittle, touching stem, bruising yellowish, then brown.

Stem: white, usually shaded with rose-pink, staining yellowish when bruised, then brown, short, stout, 3–5 inches long.

When and Where Found. Late summer to late fall, on the ground in old or second-growth Douglas fir forests, occasionally under alders.

Woodland russula   *Russula xerampelina*

Remarks. Edible, and considered by many to be the best-flavored of the Pacific Northwest's russulas. When young it is as sweet and nutty as a fresh hazelnut. Few mushrooms vary as much in cap color as this russula, but in all its chameleonlike disguises it has two constant features: the brown staining of all parts where handled or bruised and the unmistakable odor of old shrimp or crab. This odor is very strong while the mushroom is being cooked, but is dissipated by the time the cooking is finished and is absent from the flavor. Of the various color forms of *Russula xerampelina,* the two most striking are the red form, with bright scarlet cap and rose-colored stem, and variety *elaeodes,* with dark brown or olive-green cap and stem usually white or only slightly flushed with pink. *Russula olivacea* is somewhat larger than the woodland russula but similar in appearance to some forms of it. The former has an olive-green cap when young which becomes rose red to purple-red, and has a dull surface with fine wrinkles in a circular pattern. The stem is pinkish and the odor pleasant. It too is reported to be edible.

MAN-ON-HORSEBACK (Edible)
Tricholoma flavovirens (white spores)

Color and Description

Cap: canary yellow, occasionally masked with brown or reddish brown, viscid, first rounded then edge slightly upturned, 3–4 inches wide; flesh white, smelling slightly of new meal.

Gills: light yellow, not staining when bruised.

Stem: yellow to nearly white, rather short, often curved and slightly larger at the base, 3–4 inches long.

When and Where Found. Fall to frost, in mossy or sandy ground, usually under pines. Sometimes this mushroom has to be dug out of the moss or soil.

Remarks. Of good flavor and tender texture, it is one the Pacific Northwest's best edible mushrooms, easily recognized by its color and viscid cap. The similarly colored sulphur tricholoma is not viscid and has a very strong odor of coal tar gas. Another tricholoma with the same revolting odor, *T. inamoenum,* differs from the sulphur tricholoma only in being white or pallid ivory instead of yellow. Do not eat any tricholomas with this repulsive coal-tar gas odor.

Man-on-horseback   *Tricholoma flavovirens*

TIGER TRICHOLOMA (Poisonous)
Tricholoma pardinum (white spores)

Color and Description
Cap: white with fine grayish scales, first rounded then spreading, 5–10 inches wide; flesh white, firm.

Gills: white, rather close together, notched before touching the stem.

Stem: white, stout, solid, 4–5 inches long; no ring on stem.

When and Where Found. Late summer to fall seasons, on the ground in forests, often in mountain regions such as the Cascade Mountains but generally widespread.

Remarks. This is a very poisonous mushroom, causing severe, persistent gastrointestinal disturbances often requiring hospitalization. The large size, white stem and gills, and dry cap with small, spotlike grayish scales on a white ground color are its distinguishing features. There are several tricholomas with dry, scaly, gray caps that

Tiger tricholoma   *Tricholoma pardinum*

might be confused with the tiger tricholoma; they should all be avoided. Although *Tricholoma pardinum* is most frequently found in older conifer forests in the Cascade and Olympic mountains, it also occurs in second-growth stands of Douglas fir and other conifers, at sea level.

RED-BROWN TRICHOLOMA (Poisonous)
Tricholoma pessundatum (white spores)

Color and Description

Cap: dark red-brown, usually paler on the margin, smooth, slimy when wet, appearing varnished when dry, about 2–4 inches wide; flesh white, thick, firm, with strong odor of meal or of linseed oil.

Gills: white, tending to become spotted with red-brown, notched at the stem.

Stem: white, staining red-brown where handled, stout, about as long as the width of the cap or shorter.

When and Where Found. Fall, on the ground under conifers or hardwoods.

Remarks. To be avoided; has been reported as causing gastric disturbances, and compounds poisonous to laboratory animals have been detected in this mushroom. There are several tricholomas very closely related to *Tricholoma pessundatum,* all of which should be avoided. The slimy red-brown cap distinguishes them from the similarly colored *T. vaccinum.*

JAPANESE PINE MUSHROOM or MATSUTAKE (Edible)
Tricholoma (Armillaria) ponderosum (white spores)

Color and Description

Cap: white, sometimes streaked or shaded with brown, rounded then flat, up to 10 inches wide; flesh white, firm, aromatic.

Gills: white or creamy tan, becoming brownish with age, crowded together, first hidden with a white veil.

Stem: white, long, tapering to base, showing remains of thick, soft veil which usually forms a conspicuous, flaring ring.

Red-brown tricholoma   *Tricholoma pessundatum*

Japanese pine mushroom or Matsutake
Tricholoma (Armillaria) ponderosum

When and Where Found. Early to late fall, in the mountains under conifers, or along the Pacific coast under pine and in thickets of black huckleberries and rhododendrons.

Remarks. This mushroom is well known to the Japanese in the Puget Sound area. Great quantities of it are gathered every fall. By some it is considered an excellent edible species; others dislike the flavor and rather tough texture. The pungently sweet, aromatic odor is a distinguishing feature not easily forgotten once you have experienced it. A closely related species, *Tricholoma caligatum,* of smaller and more slender stature and bearing large dark scales on the cap and dark patches on the stem, is the only other mushroom in the Puget Sound area with exactly the same odor. It is also edible, but much less common than the Japanese pine mushroom. Both *Tricholoma ponderosum* and *T. caligatum* previously have been classified in the genus *Armillaria* because of the ring on their stems. Collectors interested in the pine mushroom for food should compare it closely with the white amanitas, *A. ocreata*, *A. silvicola,* and *A. smithiana* (see pages 36, 40, and 42), to avoid poisoning by these species. The correct name for the Japanese pine mushroom, *Tricholoma magnivelare,* has very seldom been used in the literature to date.

THE SANDY TRICHOLOMA (Edible)
Tricholoma populinum (white spores)

Color and Description

Cap: rather pale dingy reddish brown, smooth, viscid (but the slime layer is thin), often completely covered with sand, 3–6 inches wide; flesh white, thick, with odor and taste of fresh meal.

Gills: white, becoming spotted and stained reddish brown.

Stem: white or pallid, staining with the color of the cap where handled, becoming reddish brown below with age, short and stout, smooth.

When and Where Found. Fall, in sand under cottonwood trees. Much commoner in eastern Washington than in thè Puget Sound area.

Remarks. The name is a local one used by residents of eastern Washington and refers to the mushroom's habit of growing partly buried in the sand along rivers, under cottonwood trees. It is an edible species highly regarded by many persons, but be very careful not to confuse it with *Tricholoma pessundatum.* The two species are very similar but have different habitats. Any red-brown, viscid tricholoma with odor of meal or linseed oil, that does not grow directly under cottonwood trees, should be avoided.

The sandy tricholoma   *Tricholoma populinum*

STREAKED TRICHOLOMA (Edible)
Tricholoma portentosum (white spores)

Color and Description

Cap: nearly black in the center, sooty gray or brownish gray or often with a purplish tinge toward the margin, with fine black radiating treaks under the slimy layer, smooth, slimy when wet, 1–4 inches wide; flesh white, no special odor.

Gills: white often becoming tinged with yellow, sometimes with pale gray, notched at the stem.

Stem: white, stout, smooth.

When and Where Found. Fall, on the ground in conifer woods.

Remarks. Edible and reported to be of good quality. Remove the slimy cap surface before cooking.

SOAPY TRICHOLOMA (Edible)
Tricholoma saponaceum (white spores)

Color and Description

Cap: usually dingy greenish gray in the center, shading to pallid on the margin, but quite variable in color, smooth, 2–4 or 5 inches wide; flesh white, with odor and taste of soap or of fresh meal.

Gills: white or pallid, sometimes tinged with a dingy greenish color, deeply notched at the stem, broad, usually rather thick and well spaced.

Stem: white, or more or less flushed with the color of the cap, stout, bluntly tapered at the base, smooth; flesh white in upper part, pale pink in the base.

When and Where Found. Throughout the fall season, sometimes also in spring; on the ground in conifer woods or mixed woods of conifers and hardwoods.

Remarks. Edible, mediocre—scarcely recommendable. This is one of the commonest mushrooms of the Puget Sound area's conifer woods, but so variable in color of cap and stem that the beginner may find it difficult to recognize in all of its color forms. The pink color of the flesh in the base of the stem is seldom absent, however, and is a convenient mark of identification for this chameleonlike mushroom.

Streaked tricholoma   *Tricholoma portentosum*

Soapy tricholoma   *Tricholoma saponaceum*

Russet scaly tricholoma   *Tricholoma vaccinum*

RUSSET SCALY TRICHOLOMA (Edible)
Tricholoma vaccinum (white spores)

Color and Description

Cap: red-brown, covered with felty scales, margin inrolled at first and connected to the stem with a woolly veil that remains on the margin as the cap expands, about 2–4 inches wide; flesh white.

Gills: white or pallid, soon flecked or stained with red-brown, often more or less uniformly discolored with age.

Stem: longer than the diameter of the cap, hollow, white or pallid at the top, elsewhere spotted and streaked with red-brown fibrils.

When and Where Found. Fall, on the ground under conifers.

Remarks. Edible, but not much to recommend it. The dry scaly cap and lack of a strong odor of meal or linseed oil distinguish it from *Tricholoma pessundatum* and related species. Another very similar Tricholoma with dry scaly cap is *T. imbricatum;* its cap is duller brown and less scaly than that of *T. vaccinum,* and it lacks a shaggy marginal veil.

ZELLER'S TRICHOLOMA (Edible with caution)
Tricholoma zelleri (white spores)

Color and Description

Cap: mottled orange, olive green, and brown, or sometimes merely orange or brown, smooth, slimy when wet, shining and appearing varnished when dry, 4–8 inches wide; flesh white, firm, with odor and taste rather like fresh meal, but with an added pungent, somewhat metallic component.

Gills: white or pallid cream, becoming spotted and stained with orange-brown, attached to the stem, thin, close together.

Stem: short and thick, tapering at the base, with a flaring, ragged ring that often collapses on the stem, white or pallid above the ring, stained and mottled with brown or orange below.

When and Where Found. Fall, in conifer forests throughout the Pacific Northwest. One of the commonest mushrooms.

Remarks. Reported as edible by some authorities, but try it cautiously since there are reports of gastrointestinal upset resulting from its consumption. Most people find the odor and taste unpleasant and do not collect it for food. *Tricholoma focale* may be the correct name for this species. *Tricholoma zelleri* previously has been classified as an *Armillaria*.

Zeller's tricholoma   *Tricholoma zelleri*

Black-tufted wood tricholoma   *Tricholomopsis decora*

BLACK-TUFTED WOOD TRICHOLOMA (Edible but not
` recommended)
Tricholomopsis decora (white spores)

Color and Description

Cap: yellow, with numerous tiny black or brownish black scales all over, or only in the center, often depressed in the center, arched margin, 2–3 inches wide; flesh yellow.

Gills: yellow, squarely attached, sometimes running down the stem with a thin line.

Stem: yellow, with or without a few gray fibrils at the base, often somewhat eccentric, hollow, smooth.

When and Where Found. Fall, on conifer logs.

Remarks. Easily recognized by its yellow cap, gills, and stem, the black scales on the cap, and the growth on wood. *Tricholomopsis decora* has been listed as edible by some authors but its edibility is not well known.

RED-TUFTED WOOD TRICHOLOMA (Edible but not recommended)
Tricholomopsis rutilans (white spores)

Color and Description

Cap: at first entirely covered with purplish red fibrils that later separate into pointed scales, revealing the yellow ground color, about 3–4 inches wide; flesh yellow.

Gills: yellow, with a fine yellow fringe along the edges, as seen with a lens, notched at the stem.

Stem: yellow, with streaks and patches of purplish red fibrils, top paler yellow and lacking fibrils.

When and Where Found. Fall, on logs and stumps, or base of trees, usually conifers; typically growing attached directly to the wood.

Remarks. Edible, but not very good. The striking colors and growth on wood make this mushroom easy to recognize.

Red-tufted wood tricholoma   *Tricholomopsis rutilans*

II. Gilled mushrooms with the spore print shell pink to rosy pink to brownish salmon. A deep spore print of the latter may appear more brown than pink.

SWEETBREAD MUSHROOM (Edible)
Clitopilus prunulus (salmon pink to reddish spores)

Color and Description

Cap: dull white to grayish, dry, felty, rounded to flattened, margin uneven in age, 2–4 inches wide; flesh white; crushed flesh has on odor of meal or bread dough.

Gills: white becoming pinkish or vinaceous (light wine color) at maturity, close together, running down the stem.

Stem: dull white, 1.5–3.5 inches long, central to somewhat off-center.

When and Where Found. Single or in groups, on humus or bare soil in forested areas. Fruits in the late summer and fall seasons, widespread but usually not abundant.

Remarks. *Clitopilus prunulus* is said to be a good edible. Because of the pinkish spore color there is a danger of confusing it with the poisonous species of *Entoloma,* such as *E. lividum.* Also, it has the habit of some clitocybes, take care not to confuse it with species in this genus, which also can be poisonous.

Sweetbread mushroom *Clitopilus prunulus*

Livid entoloma *Entoloma (Rhodophyllus) lividum*

LIVID ENTOLOMA (Poisonous)
Entoloma (Rhodophyllus) lividum (pink spores)

Color and Description

Cap: dingy brown or brownish gray, rounded then flat or with a broadly raised center, smooth, soapy-feeling when wet, drying silky, 3–6 inches wide; flesh white, thick, firm, odor of fresh meal.

Gills: white, then pink from the spores, rounded where they touch the stem, broad, close together.

Stem: white, longer than the width of the cap, thick, shining, silky.

When and Where Found. Fall, on the ground in conifer or hardwood forests, or in mixed woods.

Remarks. Poisonous, causing severe gastric disturbances; it is also suspected of causing liver damage. There are several large entolomas resembling *Entoloma lividum,* some of which are edible, but distinguishing between them is a matter for a specialist in the genus; avoid all pink-spored mushrooms, especially any that look like a large tricholoma. In the Pacific Northwest the mushroom hunter's problem with large, gray-brown entolomas would be the possibility of confusing them with the fried chicken mushroom, which they resemble. Entolomas do not ordinarily grow in clusters, and they have pink gills and spores when mature (but the gills may stay white for quite a time). These features should help distinguish them from the fried chicken mushroom.

SILKY ENTOLOMA (Not recommended)
Entoloma (Rhodophyllus) sericeum (brownish salmon spores)

Color and Description

Cap: dark blackish brown when moist, silvery grayish brown when dry, bell-shaped then flat, often with the margin upturned and wavy, smooth, moist but not viscid, silky when dry, 2–3 inches wide; flesh brown when wet, drying pale, thin, fragile, with strong odor of fresh meal or of cucumbers, especially when crushed.

Gills: brownish gray, becoming flushed with browish pink from the spores, broad, deeply rounded before they touch the stem (may appear free).

Stem: same color as the cap, slender, often flattened, about as long as the width of the cap.

Silky entoloma   *Entoloma (Rhodophyllus) sericeum*

Deer mushroom   *Pluteus cervinus*

When and Where Found. Fall, and sometimes in late winter and spring, in lawns or other open grassy places.

Remarks. Said by some to be edible, but it is a good policy to avoid all pink-spored mushrooms, especially any whose gills are not truly free. This entoloma is common throughout the Pacific Northwest. Its dark brown cap and stem, strong odor of meal or cucumber, and growth in lawns are its distinguishing features.

DEER MUSHROOM (Edible)
Pluteus cervinus (pink spores)

Color and Description
Cap: dark brown through shades of tan (deer-colored), smooth, first rounded, then almost flat, 2–4 inches wide; flesh white, soft.

Gills: first white, soon pale to dark pink, soft, free from stem.

Stem: white, shaded with brown, often curved, 2–4 inches long.

When and Where Found. Early to late fall, sometimes in spring and summer; on old rotting logs or sawdust in both conifer and hardwood forests.

Remarks. The brown, smooth cap, pink gills that do not touch the stem, and habit of growing directly attached to wood or in sawdust make this an easily recognized fungus. The odor and taste are often more or less radish-like. Some consider it a fine-flavored mushroom; others find it rather inferior. Judge for yourself, but be careful not to confuse it with other pink-spored mushrooms.

SHOWY VOLVARIA (Edible)
Volvariella speciosa (flesh-pink spores)

Color and Description

Cap: pale ivory or sometimes dull buff or tinged brownish in the center, bell-shaped then rounded with a broadly raised center, smooth, slippery when wet (slightly viscid), drying to a varnished appearance, 3–6 inches wide; flesh white, thick, soft, with strong odor and taste of raw potatoes.

Gills: white at first, then pink, free from the stem, broad, thin, close together, soft.

Stem: white, long, swollen at the base, dry, dull, the base sheathed by a large, membranous, white volva with ragged, lobed edge.

When and Where Found. Fall, occasionally in the spring, on cultivated ground (flower beds, vegetable gardens, fields, compost heaps).

Remarks. Edible, but not good. In older handbooks it is listed among the poisonous species. In structure this mushroom is like the ringless amanitas (e.g., *Amanita vaginata*), but the pink spores and pink gills distinguish it.

Showy volvaria   *Volvariella speciosa*

Spring agrocybe *Agrocybe praecox*

III. Gilled mushrooms with the spore print yellow-brown, grayish brown, olive-brown, cinnamon brown, rusty brown, or bright rust color. In these brown colors there is no tinge of purple, but the difference between a brown print and a purple-brown one is often slight, and some experience is needed in order to recognize this difference.

SPRING AGROCYBE (Not recommended)
Agrocybe praecox (dark brown spores)

Color and Description

Cap: tan to brown, rounded to flattened, sometimes with a low knob in the center, smooth, dry, 1–3.5 inches wide.

Gills: attached to the stem, close together, whitish to light brown.

Stem: white overall or somewhat brownish, 2–4 inches long, moderately thick, with a more or less persistent membranous ring or zone from the veil.

When and Where Found. Fruits in the spring and early summer, in clusters or scattered to numerous, in lawns, flower beds and open woods, often on humus.

Remarks. The spring agrocybe and its relatives often are very conspicuous elements of the spring and early summer mushroom crop. Where wood chips are used, for example in flower beds, agrocybes may be very common. A smaller species, *Agrocybe pediades,* has a yellow-brown, rounded cap and a slender stem which lacks a ring. It commonly occurs in lawns and other grassy areas. Since brown-spored spring mushrooms are not well known and are easily confused, none are recommended for the table.

DEADLY CONOCYBE (Deadly poisonous)
Conocybe filaris (cinnamon-brown spores)

Color and Description

Cap: yellow-brown to orange-brown or reddish-orange brown, moist to dry, smooth, margin with radiating lines, cone-shaped to rounded or flat, often with central knob, .25–1.5 inches wide; flesh thin.

Gills: off-white becoming rust brown, close together, attached to the stem.

Stem: 1–2 inches long, slender, yellowish to yellow-brown or orange-brown, with a membranous, fragile, movable, and nonpersistent ring from the partial veil.

When and Where Found. Widespread, fruiting in the late summer and fall. Found scattered or in groups on decayed wood, wood and bark chips and in lawns and grassy areas.

Remarks. The deadly conocybe is one of many small brown-spored mushrooms in the west. It is similar in appearance to certain galerinas, such as *Galerina autumnalis,* both contain the deadly amanita toxin. *Conocybe filaris* and the deadly galerinas may occur with hallucinogenic species of *Psilocybe.* Certain psilocybes, such as *Psilocybe stuntzii,* can be confused with these deadly species. *Don't eat any small, brown-spored mushrooms. Conocybe filaris* also has been called *Pholiotina filaris* in recent literature.

The brown dunce cap, *Conocybe tenera,* is another fairly common conocybe characterized by a brown, cone- to bell-shaped cap, cinnamon gills, and a long slender stem which lacks a ring. It occurs in grassy areas, such as lawns, and in wooded areas and is widespread in North America.

Deadly conocybe *Conocybe filaris*

PURPLE-STAINING CORTINARIUS (Not recommended)
Cortinarius mutabilis (rusty brown spores)

Color and Description

Cap: violet or grayish violet, becoming somewhat mottled with buff or pale brown on the center of older caps, smooth, viscid, 2–4 inches wide; flesh violet, changing to dark purple where bruised, no special odor or taste.

Gills: violet when young, becoming brown with spores, changing to dark violet or purple where bruised, rounded before they touch the stem.

Stem: same color as the cap, staining dark purple or violet where bruised, dry, silky, bearing the remains of the violet cortina on its upper part, a little longer than the width of the cap, thickened below into a club-shaped bulb.

When and Where Found. Fall, on the ground in conifer forests, especially in the mountains.

Purple-staining cortinarius   *Cortinarius mutabilis*

Remarks. This is a common cortinarius of the Cascade and Olympic mountains, recognizable by its violet colors, sticky cap, and especially the dark purple color assumed by the bruised flesh of all parts. It and its relatives are not recommended for eating.

THE WESTERN RED-CAPPED CORTINARIUS (Not recommended)
Cortinarius phoeniceus var. *occidentalis* (rusty brown spores)

Color and Description
Cap: rich red, sometimes developing brownish tones in age or as the red color fades, dry to moist, rounded to flattened, 1–4 inches wide; flesh red to olive brown.

Gills: rich red to purplish red, with a changeable sheen when viewed at different angles.

The western red-capped cortinarius
Cortinarius phoeniceus var. *occidentalis*

Stem: yellow with yellowish or slightly reddish fibrils from the veil, base often tinged reddish.

When and Where Found. Late summer into winter, appearing earliest in the higher mountains. In conifer or mixed woods, on the ground, often in groups.

Remarks. The red cap and gills on a predominately yellow stem distinguish this beautiful cortinarius. Its close relative, *Cortinarius semisanguineus,* has a yellow-brown cap but otherwise is similar in appearance. Neither is recommended for eating since they are somewhat related to species which contain the toxic compounds cortinarin A and B. See the section on orellanine in the chapter on mushroom poisons.

THE PUNGENT CORTINARIUS (Not recommended)
Cortinarius traganus (rusty brown spores)

Color and Description

Cap: bright lilac-purple, sometimes discoloring whitish, dry, silky, rounded to nearly flattened, 2–5 inches wide; flesh yellow-brown; odor strong, often unpleasant, but in some forms fruity and pleasant.

Gills: yellow-brown, cinnamon or reddish cinnamon-brown, at times slightly purplish, covered at first by a lilac cobwebby veil.

Stem: bright lilac-purple, sometimes with whitish areas, silky, enlarged towards the base, 2–5 inches long, up to 2 inches thick.

When and Where Found. Usually fruiting in the fall season under conifers. On the ground in needles but often found in moss; widespread and common.

Remarks. The pungent cortinarius is easily recognized by its rather large size, beautiful silky lilac cap and stem surfaces, yellow-brown flesh, and strong odor. The fruit bodies of this species usually have a fairly strong, pungent penetrating odor. Some forms have a spicy or fragrant odor, like overripe pears. A similar species, *Cortinarius pyriodorus,* has lilac flesh, lilac gills at first, and often a fragrant odor. None of these is recommended for eating.

THE VIOLET CORTINARIUS (Edible)
Cortinarius violaceus (rusty brown spores)

Color and Description

Cap: deep purple, roughened by small dry scales, rounded then flat, 2–5 inches wide; flesh purplish, firm.

Gills: purple, then rusty brown with spores, cobwebby veil present on young specimens.

Stem: purple, fibrous, showing slight remains of cobwebby veil.

When and Where Found. Fall, on the ground in fir needles in old Douglas fir forests.

Remarks. Edible but becomes quite dark when cooked. There are many other purple *Cortinarii*, but the violet cortinarius is known by the dry, rough cap which, when old, has an almost metallic sheen.

The pungent cortinarius   *Cortinarius traganus*

The violet cortinarius   *Cortinarius violaceus*

Autumnal galerina *Galerina autumnalis*

AUTUMNAL GALERINA (Poisonous)
Galerina autumnalis (rusty brown spores)

Color and Description

Cap: yellow-brown when wet, fading to buff when dry, rounded often with a small central knob, smooth, sticky when wet (slightly viscid), 1–1.5 inches wide; flesh watery brown when moist, pale buff when dry, thin, without special odor or with slight odor and taste of cucumber.

Gills: pale brown at first, then darker brown from the spores, touching the stem.

Stem: pale brown, then darker brown from the base up with age, slender, hollow, rather tough, smooth or roughened with fibrils up to the thin, narrow, white ring.

When and Where Found. Fall, growing solitary or in small clusters on wood, or seemingly on the ground but from buried wood; both in the woods and in open areas outside them.

Remarks. Poisonous; this very dangerous mushroom contains amatoxins, the deadly amanita toxins. A similar species (*Galerina* *venenata*) nearly caused the death of a couple in Portland, Oregon, who found them growing in a lawn, and once it also caused the death of a Washington teenager who mistook it for a hallucinogenic *Psilocybe*. Compare, for example, *Psilocybe stuntzii*. Fortunately, most mushroom hunters seem little inclined to collect small, brown mushrooms such as these for the table. The sticky, yellow-brown cap, dark brown stem with its narrow white ring, and growth on wood are the features to watch for in recognizing and avoiding this galerina.

BIG LAUGHING GYMNOPILUS (Hallucinogenic)
Gymnopilus spectabilis (orange to rusty brown spores)

Color and Description
Cap: light orange-yellow to ochre-orange, rounded to nearly flattened, the center sometimes with a knob, smooth or with small scales, dry, large, 3–7 inches wide; flesh thick, light yellow, very bitter taste.

Gills: pale yellow to orangish then rusty, crowded together,

Big laughing gymnopilus   *Gymnopilus spectabilis*

squarely attached to the stem or running down it slightly.

Stem: same color as the cap or more brownish at the base, 2–8 inches long, thick; veil membranous leaving a yellowish, superior, persisting ring, or the ring collapsing or veil forming only a zone on the upper stem.

When and Where Found. In clusters, often very large ones, on logs, stumps, or from buried wood. Widespread and fruiting in the late summer and fall seasons.

Remarks. This beautiful mushroom is inedible because of its very bitter taste. In spite of the bitter taste, it has apparently been eaten by some individuals and has caused hallucinations. It contains the same compounds as the hallucinogenic psilocybes. The name big laughing gymnopilus (mushroom) comes from Japan, where it has been reported to cause "unmotivated laughter and foolish behavior."

POISON PIE (Poisonous)
Hebeloma crustuliniforme (dull brown spores)

Color and Description
Cap: pale cream color to pale crust brown, smooth, slimy-viscid when wet, about 2–4 inches wide; flesh white, thick, with odor of radish.

Gills: white then dull brown, with white edges, notched where they touch the stem, thin, close together.

Stem: white, dry, slightly granular at least at the top, as long as the

Poison pie   *Hebeloma crustuliniforme*

width of the cap or longer, usually with a bulb at the base.

When and Where Found. Throughout the fall season, on the ground especially in conifer forests, but also in mixed stands. It often forms large fairy rings.

Remarks. Poisonous; it causes gastric disturbances and may have other more harmful effects. It is a very common mushroom of the Pacific Northwest's conifer forests, recognizable by the slimy pale cap, white stem, dull brown gills, and radish odor.

DARK-CENTERED HEBELOMA (Probably poisonous)
Hebeloma mesophaeum (dull brown spores)

Color and Description

Cap: dark brown at the center, shading to pallid on the margin, usually rounded or with a low knob at the center, smooth, viscid, with remnants of the fibrous veil on the margin, about 2 inches wide, rarely more; flesh white, thin, with slight to strong odor of radish.

Gills: white then dull brown, thin, close together, notched at the stem.

Stem: white at the top, becoming dark, dull brown from the base upward, slender, streaked with loose fibrils in the lower part, usually longer than the width of the cap.

When and Where Found. Fall, on the ground under all kinds of trees, but mostly in conifer woods.

Remarks. To be avoided; it does not have as bad a reputation as the

Dark-centered hebeloma   *Hebeloma mesophaeum*

poison pie, but is suspected of causing poisonings. It is usually one of the commonest hebelomas, especially in conifer woods. The brown-centered cap with marginal veil patches and the usually rather faint radish odor are distinctive.

TORN-CAPPED INOCYBE (Poisonous)
Inocybe lacera (brown spores)

Color and Description

Cap: medium to dark brown, the center sometimes darker than the margin, rounded to flattened or the center with a slight knob, dry, scaly, usually shaggy or torn, .5–1.5 inches wide; flesh thin, white or slightly brownish; odor disagreeable or pungent or like chestnut catkins.

Gills: medium brown, the edges sometimes paler, close together, squarely attached or notched at the stem.

Stem: whitish to brownish tinged or slightly pinkish above, medium to dark brown below, the base sometimes blackish, with surface fibrils, .75–2 inches long; veil cobwebby, soon disappearing.

When and Where Found. Spring, summer and fall seasons; on

Torn-capped inocybe   *Inocybe lacera*

the ground, in soil, needles or moss, usually in groups, frequently along paths, roads or in open places; widespread and sometimes common.

Remarks. This little brown inocybe, the classical little brown mushroom, fruits at all times of the year when conditions of moisture and temperature are favorable. It and its relatives contain muscarine and are very toxic. Avoid all little brown mushrooms; they are often toxic and consistently difficult to identify.

TURNIP-BULB INOCYBE (Poisonous)
Inocybe napipes (dull brown spores)

Color and Description
Cap: dark brown, sometimes with a silvery superficial coating that tends to hide the color, bell-shaped then flat or slightly rounded, with pronounced central knob, smooth, soapy-feeling but not viscid when wet, drying silky, 1.5–3 inches wide; flesh white, thin, firm, with unpleasant odor of chestnut catkins.

Gills: white at first, then dull grayish brown, touching the stem.

Turnip-bulb inocybe   *Inocybe napipes*

Stem: pallid at the top, brown below, satiny, rigid, with a turnip-like bulb at the base, usually longer than the width of the cap.

When and Where Found. Fall, also in the spring in some seasons, on the ground under conifers.

Remarks. Very poisonous; a few fruiting bodies could contain enough muscarine to cause a severe case of poisoning requiring immediate medical attention. Fortunately, the unprepossessing appearance and unpleasant odor are apt to discourage the would-be mycophagist.

BLUSHING INOCYBE (Poisonous)
Inocybe pudica (dull brown spores)

Color and Description

Cap: white, becoming more or less flushed with salmon pink or red with age, bell-shaped, slippery when wet but not truly viscid, 1–2 inches wide; flesh white, with unpleasant odor of chestnut catkins.

Gills: white, often becoming flushed with pink or red, eventually dull brown from the spores, notched at the stem.

Blushing inocybe   *Inocybe pudica*

Stem: white, staining like the gills and cap, slender, dry, silky, with or without a slight bulb at the base.

When and Where Found. Throughout the fall season, in conifer woods.

Remarks. To be avoided, like all inocybes. This very common species is easy to recognize if the red staining is pronounced, as it often is, but sometimes there is only a hint of it around the edge of the cap. Very similar species are *I. geophylla,* with sharp-pointed, pure white cap and stem that never stain red, and *I. lilacina,* with lilac cap that fades to dingy cream color with age.

COMMON PAXILLUS (Poisonous)
Paxillus involutus (yellow-brown spores)

Color and Description
Cap: yellow-brown to dark brown, sometimes staining red brown in age or when bruised, rounded then flat, finally shallowly funnel-shaped, margin inrolled at first and long remaining so, finally flat, often with riblike markings, with smooth, matted-woolly surface that is sticky when wet, 4–8 inches wide, occasionally larger; flesh buff to brownish yellow, thick, somewhat sour taste.

Common paxillus   *Paxillus involutus*

Gills: yellow then brown, staining brown to red-brown where bruised, running down the stem, close together, often with cross veins.

Stem: about the same color as the cap, thick, smooth, dry, usually shorter than the width of the cap.

When and Where Found. Late summer and fall, on the ground in woods or in open places. It frequently grows in lawns, usually under or near trees.

Remarks. This is one of the most common mushrooms within the city limits. It was long considered edible, and probably is still eaten by some individuals. Some persons cannot tolerate it, especially if it is not thoroughly cooked. If eaten raw it is apt to cause serious gastric disturbances. Also, there are reports that it produces a gradually acquired hypersensitivity that causes kidney failure.

KAUFFMAN'S PHAEOCOLLYBIA (Edibility unknown)
Phaeocollybia kauffmanii (pale cinnamon-brown spores)

Color and Description

Cap: cinnamon, pinkish cinnamon to dark red-brown, fading to reddish or apricot orange, obtuse then expanded, the center often with a rounded knob or flattened, the edge persistently inrolled, slimy to viscid, 3–6 or up to 10 inches wide; flesh has a thick cartilaginous rind at the surface; meal-like taste and odor.

Gills: dirty whitish to grayish orange-brown when mature, slightly attached to nearly free from the stem, crowded together.

Stem: pinkish buff above, dingy purplish brown below, darkening in age, 8–16 inches long, tapering downward to a long rootlike projection, thick at the top; interior with a thick cartilaginous rind and a soft, pallid center; no veil.

When and Where Found. Fruits in the late summer and fall seasons; scattered or in groups under conifers, mainly on the coast in the Pacific Northwest, especially in the Sitka spruce zone; moderately common.

Remarks. Several different phaeocollybias occur in the Pacific Northwest and Kauffman's phaeocollybia simply serves as an example of the genus. This is a large species; many are smaller and grow

Kauffman's phaeocollybia   *Phaeocollybia kauffmanii*

scattered or others occur in clusters of many fruit bodies. The edibility of phaeocollybias is unknown. Since many brown-spored mushrooms are toxic and their identification difficult, it is best not to experiment. The cartilaginous texture and often disagreeable taste deter most persons from eating them.

GOLDEN FALSE PHOLIOTA (Edible with caution)
Phaeolepiota aurea (ocher spores)

Color and Description

Cap: light gold or leather brown, grainy or suede-like, covered with a powdery material that rubs off when dry, first rounded then expanded, 4–14 inches wide; flesh whitish yellow, odor pleasantly aromatic, somewhat like bitter almonds.

Golden false pholiota   *Phaeolepiota aurea*

Gills: yellowish brown, first covered by a sheathing veil which, on breaking, forms a ring on the stem.

Stem: brown, fibrous, showing a distinct ring, below which it is covered with the same powdery material that is on the cap.

When and Where Found. Fall, on the ground in old-growth Douglas fir forests, or on their edges under alders.

Remarks. A large, handsome mushroom not easily confused with any other. It is an edible species for some individuals but others are made sick by it. Do not eat a large quantity when trying it for the first time. Discard the stems.

LEMON-YELLOW PHOLIOTA (Edible with caution)
Pholiota limonella (brown spores)

Color and Description

Cap: yellow to yellow-orange with a yellow-brown center, viscid, covered with red-brown to brown semierect scales, 3–5 inches wide; flesh yellow or paler.

Gills: yellowish, first covered with a veil which, on breaking, partially adheres to the edge of the cap, forming a small ring on the stem.

Stem: cream-buff to light yellow with a slight ring, dry, covered from ring to base with dry, yellow to brownish yellow or red-brown scales.

When and Where Found. Fall, in dense groups and clusters, usually on rotting logs and trees of hardwood, especially maple, some forms also on compost; sometimes in wounds in live trees. Sometimes hundreds cluster on one log.

Remarks. Edible with caution since it causes gastric disturbances in some people. Usually of poor quality, tasting like a marshmallow without sugar. The rough pholiota and the bristly pholiota are similar species. The lemon-yellow pholiota is distinguished by its yellow color, slimy cap, dry, scaly stem, and clustered growth on logs or stumps. The scales on the cap may be dry at first, but they soon become sticky or gluey. The name *Pholiota squarroso-adiposa* also has been applied to this species.

Lemon-yellow pholiota   *Pholiota limonella*

Bristly pholiota *Pholiota squarrosoides*

BRISTLY PHOLIOTA (Edible)
Pholiota squarrosoides (brown spores)

Color and Description

Cap: cream-white, covered with erect, pointed, triangular, tawny scales, under which the true surface of the cap is viscid, 3–5 inches wide; flesh white, often with an agreeable odor of cinnamon rolls.

Gills. whitish, then brownish tan, first covered with veil which, on breaking, hangs in points from the edge of the cap and forms a ragged ring on the stem.

Stem: whitish, then brownish tan, covered below the ring with tawny scales.

When and Where Found. Late fall, on fallen logs or dead trunks of both alder and maple in old Douglas fir forests.

Remarks. Edible. Be sure to remove the bristly scales. The scaly pholiota, *Pholiota squarrosa,* and the lemon yellow pholiota, *Pholiota limonella,* are similar species.

TERRESTRIAL PHOLIOTA (Edible)
Pholiota terrestris (dark cinnamon-brown spores)

Color and Description

Cap: brown, covered with dark brown, pointed, dry scales on a viscid, paler dingy brown or brownish yellow surface, the scales also becoming viscid in wet weather, rounded then flat, about 1–4 inches wide; flesh buff or brown, soft, no special odor or taste.

Gills: pallid at first, then cinnamon-brown, thin, close together, attached to the stem.

Terrestrial pholiota   *Pholiota terrestris*

Stem: dingy ivory to buff, usually becoming brown toward the base, covered with small, dark brown scales up to the bandlike, fibrillose ring, slender, dry, longer than the width of the cap.

When and Where Found. Fall, sometimes also in spring, on the ground, usually in clusters of many individuals. It seems to prefer open places such as paths or abandoned roadways or clearings in the woods, and sometimes grows in lawns or other cultivated areas.

Remarks. This pholiota grows abundantly throughout the Pacific Northwest, and is one of the first mushrooms the novice is apt to encounter. It is not always easy to recognize because of considerable variation in size, scaliness, and color; the scales, for instance, are easily rubbed or washed off, leaving a smooth cap quite different in appearance from the normal scaly condition. It is an edible mushroom, but opinions on its desirability differ. Being often available in quantity, it is worth trying; if you like it, you can certainly eat your fill.

GYPSY MUSHROOM (Edible)
Rozites caperata (brown spores)

Color and Description
Cap: warm tan, with a thin, white, hoary coating at first, wrinkled or even corrugated, seldom smooth, rounded then flat, 2–5 inches wide; flesh white, firm.

Gills: pale tan, often banded with darker and lighter brown, irregular, just touching the stem; at first covered with a white veil which, on breaking, forms a ring on the stem.

Stem: pale tan, showing remains of veil as a ring.

When and Where Found. Late summer to late fall, on the ground in conifer forests, often found in Douglas fir forests at lower levels in the Cascade and Olympic mountains.

Remarks. This mushroom is well known in Europe and often sold in markets there. It is an excellent edible species which should be better known. The hoary coating of the cap may not be very apparent if the cap is wet or if the specimen is old. In fruiting bodies in prime condition, however, that and the curious color banding of the gills are distinctive features.

Gypsy mushroom *Rozites caperata*

IV. Gilled mushrooms with the spore print dark reddish chocolate, purple-brown, brownish purple, grayish purple, purplish black, or black. These colors are referred to as purple-brown or black in most mushroom handbooks. The eye needs some training to distinguish between the reddish chocolate color and some of the richer browns of the brown-spored group.

THE PRINCE (Edible)
Agaricus augustus (purple-brown spores)

Color and Description
Cap: cream-white or light tan, staining yellow then orange-brown with age or where handled, covered with close-pressed, small, reddish

brown scales, rounded then flat, 5–17 inches wide; flesh white, aromatic, almond odor.

Gills: first cream white, then dull rose, becoming purplish brown, in early stages covered with a thick white veil which, on breaking, forms a large ring on stem.

Stem: cream-white shaded with brown, larger at base, 5–12 inches long.

When and Where Found. In rainy seasons from June to October, in dry seasons beginning to fruit in August. If the place in which it appears is watered, successive crops will be produced. Often grows near compost heaps or in flower beds, on lawns, in orchards, sometimes near edges of roads, usually in the open.

Remarks. One of the most desirable of edible mushrooms, meaty and of fine flavor. Be careful to distinguish this mushroom from *Agaricus praeclarisquamosus* and *Agaricus hondensis,* which cause severe gastrointestinal poisoning in most individuals.

MEADOW MUSHROOM (Edible)
Agaricus campestris (purple-brown spores)

Color and Description
Cap: cream white, silky-smooth or occasionally with small scales, first rounded then flat, 3–6 inches wide; flesh white, firm.

Gills: pink, then purple-brown, at first covered with white veil that forms a slight ring on the stem on breaking.

Stem: white, occasionally shaded rose, short, pointed at the base, 3–5 inches long.

When and Where Found. Spring, summer and fall; east of the Cascade Mountains most often in the spring. In open meadows, lawns, golf courses, parking strips; always in the open, never in the woods.

Remarks. Holds top honors with the morel, king boletus, and yellow chanterelle as an edible mushroom. The silky white cap, thin ragged ring, bright pink young gills, and growth in open, grassy places are its distinguishing features. Contrary to popular belief, the meadow mushroom is not the commercially cultivated mushroom.

The prince   *Agaricus augustus*

Meadow mushroom   *Agaricus campestris*

Felt-ringed agaricus   *Agaricus hondensis*

FELT-RINGED AGARICUS (Poisonous)
Agaricus hondensis (purplish chocolate spores)

Color and Description

Cap: covered with thin, rather broad, flat, "ironed-down" pale fawn-colored or pale lilac-brown scales on a white or ivory ground color, tending to become somewhat darker in age, convex then flat, smooth, dry, 4–6 inches wide, sometimes larger; flesh white, thick, no special odor, or sometimes smelling of creosote.

Gills: usually pink at first, sometimes pale grayish lilac, finally chocolate brown, free, rounded at the stem, thin, close together.

Stem: white, sometimes turning yellow near the base, stout, with a bulb at the base, smooth, satiny, about as long as the width of the cap; ring flaring, smooth above, felty below, with thick, even edge.

When and Where Found. Fall, on the ground, often in deep litter, under conifers, mostly Douglas fir and hemlock.

Remarks. This handsome agaricus looks as though it should be an excellent edible species, but it develops a strong creosote odor in cooking and has a most unpleasant, soapy-metallic flavor with over-tones of creosote. Apparently it is toxic to almost everyone, causing severe gastrointestinal poisoning.

Snowy cap   *Agaricus nivescens*

SNOWY CAP (Edible)
Agaricus nivescens (dark purplish chocolate spores)

Color and Description

Cap: white, eventually pale buff in the center when old, rounded, dry, silky-smooth at the center, with a few scales at the margin, 3–5 inches wide; flesh white, not changing color where broken, thick, firm, almond odor.

Gills: white in unopened buttons, then pale grayish or brownish lilac, finally chocolate brown, free from the stem, rather narrow.

Stem: white, thick, with a bulb at the base, silky smooth in the upper part, with tiny pointed scales or warts in an area just above the bulb, about as long as the width of the cap; ring white, thick, flaring, with triangular felty patches on its undersurface.

When and Where Found. Fall, in grassy places near trees.

Remarks. Edible and of good quality. This agaricus seems to be rather common in the Puget Sound area and is probably often mistaken for the woodland mushroom, which it resembles. The small, pointed scales above the bulb on the stem and the failure of cap or stem to turn yellow where bruised are its distinctive features.

Flat-topped mushroom *Agaricus praeclarisquamosus*

FLAT-TOPPED MUSHROOM (Poisonous)
Agaricus praeclarisquamosus (purplish chocolate spores)

Color and Description

Cap: silvery gray to dark grayish brown, darker in center, smooth, with light to dark gray-brown flat to upturned scales, first rounded then spreading flat, 3–6 inches wide; flesh white, darkening to pinkish with age, frequently smelling like creosote.

Gills: pale pink, then bright pink, turning purple-brown, first hidden by a white veil which, on breaking, forms a distinct ring on the stem.

Stem: white, then dull pinkish, usually staining bright yellow below when cut or bruised, slightly larger at the base, 3–5 inches long, often clustered.

When and Where Found. Fall, on the ground under deciduous trees and conifers.

Remarks. The flat-top mushroom is a tempting specimen for the hunter, but it is toxic to most individuals, causing severe gastrointestinal poisoning. Specimens that smell of creosote (phenol) are particularly likely to cause illness, and even those with a normal mushroom smell can be poisonous. It is wise, therefore, to avoid eating this mushroom. *Agaricus meleagris* is another name that has been used for this mushroom. *Agaricus placomyces* is a similar species found in eastern North America.

SYLVAN AGARICUS (Edible with caution)
Agaricus silvaticus (purplish chocolate spores)

Color and Description

Cap: covered with small, russet, tawny, or red-brown, "ironed-down" scales, rounded or flat, dry, smooth, 2–6 inches wide; flesh white, thick, firm, no special odor, slowly turning reddish brown where cut open.

Gills: whitish at first, then pale pink, finally chocolate brown, free, rounded at the stem, thin, crowded together.

Stem: white, often tinged brownish pink, and flushed with dingy brown in age, smooth, satiny, usually with a bulb at the base, as long as the width of the cap; ring white, ample, thin.

When and Where Found. Fall, under conifers or hardwoods; typically in forests.

Remarks. Edible and considered good by many, but it does not agree with everyone and should be tried cautiously at first. For many

Sylvan agaricus   *Agaricus silvaticus*

years we have called it *Agaricus silvaticus,* but it is not the true *A. silvaticus* of Europe, which European authorities agree is a species with red-staining flesh. Until the western *"silvaticus"* is officially named, there seems little harm in keeping the name it has long had. It closely resembles the flat-topped mushroom, but has red-brown instead of gray-brown scales, lacks the smell of creosote, and has a thinner, wider ring. In the color of its scales it resembles the prince, but it does not stain yellow and does not have an almond odor.

WOODLAND MUSHROOM (Edible with caution)
Agaricus silvicola (purple-brown spores)

Color and Description

Cap: white, smooth, silky, rounded then flat, sometimes staining yellow when bruised, 3–5 inches wide; flesh white, almond odor.

Gills: pink, turning purple-brown, first concealed by a white veil which, on breaking, forms a thick ring on the stem.

Stem: white, often abruptly bulbous at the base, 3–5 inches long.

When and Where Found. Fall, occasionally in the spring, on the ground in Douglas fir and spruce forests.

Remarks. Widely recognized as an edible mushroom, but it should be tried with caution the first time, as it is known to be poisonous to some persons and not to others. There are several other large white species of *Agaricus* that easily can be mistaken for the woodland mushroom. One of these, the prairie mushroom (*A. arven-*

Woodland mushroom   *Agaricus silvicola*

sis), once common in the Puget Sound area but now seldom found, is larger, fleshier, and has larger spores than *A. silvicola,* but is otherwise very similar, and is edible if the same precautions are taken. Two others, *A. albolutescens* and *A. xanthodermus,* can cause severe gastric disturbances. They can be recognized by the intense yellow stain that appears instantly whenever their flesh is bruised or even touched. In addition, *A. xanthodermus* has a strong smell of creosote. The woodland mushroom also stains yellow, but much more slowly and much less intensely than these two.

WOOLLY-STEMMED AGARICUS (Edible)
Agaricus subrutilescens (purplish chocolate spores)

Color and Description
Cap: covered with rather large, brownish purple, flat scales which may become somewhat reddish tinged in age, smooth, dry, 4–6 inches wide; flesh white, thick, rather soft, odor not distinctive or fruity to spicy upon cutting, no color change where bruised.

Gills: bright pink at first, then chocolate brown, rounded and free at the stem, thin, close together.

Stem: pure white, slightly thickened toward the base, with a thin, membranous white ring, satiny above the ring, densely covered below with patches and streaks of white woolly substance, about as long as the width of the cap.

When and Where Found. Fall, under conifers or in mixed stands

Woolly-stemmed agaricus   *Agaricus subrutilescens*

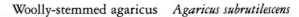

of hardwoods and conifers. It is uncommon north of Olympia, Washington, more abundant farther south, and fairly common in Oregon and northern California.

Remarks. Edible and choice. The conspicuous purplish brown scales on the cap and the white woolly stem make it easy to recognize.

COLORFUL GOMPHIDIUS (Edible)
Chroogomphus (Gomphidius) rutilus (black spores)

Color and Description

Cap: olive-brown or wine brown or tawny, sometimes orange-ocher, often wine red in old specimens, rounded, sometimes bluntly pointed in the center, smooth, sticky but not slimy, soon dry and shining, 2–3 inches wide; flesh pale orange, thick, no special taste or odor.

Gills: buff to yellowish brown or cinnamon-brown at first, soon gray from the spores, running down the stem.

Stem: buff or orange-buff, becoming wine red in age, longer than the width of the cap, tapering at the base.

When and Where Found. Fall, on the ground under lodgepole or ponderosa pine, sometimes also other conifers.

Remarks. Edible. The slightly sticky cap and the mixtures of orange, buff, wine red, and brown are distinctive.

WOOLLY GOMPHIDIUS (Edible)
Chroogomphus (Gomphidius) tomentosus (black spores)

Color and Description

Cap: orange or orange buff, rounded or flat, dry, felted or finely and densely woolly, 1–3 inches wide; flesh orange buff, thin, soft, no special odor.

Gills: pale orange, then gray or grayish orange from the spores, running down the stem, thick, well spaced.

Stem: orange or orange-buff, slender, narrowing toward the base, dry, dull, felted below like the cap surface, 2–7 inches long.

When and Where Found. Fall, in conifer woods, especially in the mountains. Abundant in some seasons, difficult to find in others.

Colorful gomphidius   *Chroogomphus (Gomphidius) rutilus*

Woolly gomphidius   *Chroogomphus (Gomphidius) tomentosus*

Remarks. This is a characteristic mushroom of the Pacific Northwestern conifer forests. The dry, felted, orange cap distinguishes it. Purple stains sometimes develop in older specimens. Although it must have been tried at one time or another, we have no authentic reports on its quality as an edible.

ALCOHOL INKY CAP (Edible with caution)
Coprinus atramentarius (black spores)

Color and Description

Cap: lead gray or grayish tan, oval with depressed lines on the surface, 2–4 inches wide; flesh grayish to tannish white.

Gills: grayish, soon melting into black fluid.

Stem: white, hollow, splitting, often with a slight ring or zone of grayish fibrils on the base.

When and Where Found. Spring or fall, on the ground, densely clustered, often on the edges of roads or fields, sometimes on lawns.

Remarks. Edible but not as good as the shaggy mane. Only very young specimens should be eaten. Never drink alcohol when eating this inky cap, or for five days afterward. See the chapter on mushroom poisons.

Alcohol inky cap   *Coprinus atramentarius*

Shaggy mane   *Coprinus comatus*

SHAGGY MANE (Edible)
Coprinus comatus (black spores)

Color and Description

Cap: white to light reddish brown or somewhat gray in age, covered, except at the center, with scales that bend back, narrowly cylindric, appearing like a closed umbrella on its handle, spreading with age, 4–12 inches high; flesh white at first, then darkening.

Gills: white shading to pink, in flat folds against the stem, turning grey then black as spores develop, and melting into a black fluid.

Stem: white, hollow, with small movable ring, slightly thicker at the base, 4–10 inches long.

When and Where Found. Spring or fall after rain; in the open, on the ground, in gravel by roadsides, near garbage dumps, or in decaying sawdust near old logging roads.

Remarks. A well-known, edible mushroom of good flavor and consistency when young. Easily distinguished from other inky caps by its height and conspicuously scaly cap.

SHINY CAP (Edible)
Coprinus micaceus (black spores)

Color and Description

Cap: brownish tan to ocher yellow, at first covered with tiny glistening particles which disappear in age, oval with lines on edge, later spreading, 2–3 inches wide; flesh whitish, thin.

Gills: grayish white, soon black with spores.

Stem: white, fragile, hollow, 3–4 inches long.

When and Where Found. Spring and fall, at the base of old trees or from decayed wood underground, usually in the open.

Remarks. Small mushroom, but has an excellent flavor in sauces. It is called "shiny cap" because the mealy particles on the cap glisten like mica.

OREGON GOMPHIDIUS (Edible)
Gomphidius oregonensis (blackish brown spores)

Color and Description

Cap: dingy white to dingy salmon pink or gray mixed with reddish brown, rounded, slimy, often with soil particles stuck to surface, 1–6 inches wide; flesh thick at the center, white or tinted with cap colors.

Gills: white to smoke gray, well spaced, running down the stem, soft and waxy in appearance.

Stem: white above ring left by the separation of the slime veil, lower surface yellowish or deep yellow to the base, slimy below the ring, 1.5–3 inches long, fairly stout, tapered slightly to base; flesh white above, yellow in base.

When and Where Found. Found in the late summer and fall seasons under conifers, frequently with Douglas fir. Typically grows in clusters from deep in the soil; some fruit bodies may be aborted.

Remarks. The Oregon gomphidius is edible but not often collected for food because of its dingy appearance and soil-coated cap and stem surfaces. It is very similar in appearance to the slimy gomphidius, *Gomphidius glutinosus*; this species, however, usually does not grow in clusters from deep in the soil. The cap color of the slimy gomphidius may be more purplish than that of the Oregon

Shiny cap *Coprinus micaceus*

Oregon gomphidius *Gomphidius oregonensis*

gomphidius, but the two overlap in color range and may be difficult to distinguish by field characteristics alone. Both are edible, however, so the question from that standpoint is academic.

ROSY GOMPHIDIUS (Edible)
Gomphidius subroseus (blackish brown spores)

Color and Description
Cap: rose-pink, rounded then spreading, surface covered by a thick, gelatinous covering, slimy when wet, 2–4 inches wide; flesh white.

Gills: whitish, then gray, soft and waxy, running down the stem.

Stem: white, yellow at the tapering base, 2–3 inches long.

When and Where Found. Fall, on the ground, often in moss, frequently in Douglas fir forests.

Remarks. This easily identified mushroom grows prolifically in many parts of the Puget Sound area and also at low elevations in the Cascade and Olympic mountains. The gelatinous covering is easily stripped from the caps. Although considered a choice edible mushroom by some, it does not have much flavor.

SMOKY-GILLED WOODLOVER (Edible)
Naematoloma capnoides (purple-brown spores)

Color and Description
Cap: ocher yellow, at times more orange to cinnamon in the center, moist but not viscid, rounded then flat, 2–3 inches wide; flesh whitish, quite firm, mild taste.

Gills: white to smoky gray then purple-brown, touching the stem.

Stem: white, becoming darker at the base, showing a few traces of the veil.

When and Where Found. Early to late fall, on decaying logs in the forest, in clusters or in rows.

Remarks. Edible and distinguished from the bitter, green-gilled woodlover, *Naematoloma fasciculare,* by the smoky gray gills, as well as the lack of a bitter taste. It is rarely abundant until near the end of the season, and often continues to appear after cold weather has discouraged most other fungi.

Rosy gomphidius *Gomphidius subroseus*

Smoky-gilled woodlover *Naematoloma capnoides*

Clustered woodlover *Naematoloma fasciculare*

CLUSTERED WOODLOVER (Poisonous)
Naematoloma fasciculare (purple-brown spores)

Color and Description

Cap: orange-yellow or greenish yellow, first rounded, later flat, turning olive-green when rain-soaked, 2–3 inches wide; flesh yellowish, very bitter.

Gills: at first yellow, then somewhat greenish, finally purplish.

Stem: yellow, often twisted because of the dense, clustered growth.

When and Where Found. Fall, occasionally in the spring or winter, on dead trees or stumps everywhere in the forest or along the edge of woodlands.

Remarks. This mushroom, also called the sulfur tuft, is most attractive, but is considered poisonous. However, its exceedingly bitter taste, not lost in cooking, will deter the gatherer. Compare the smoky-gilled woodlover.

HAYMAKER'S MUSHROOM (Not recommended, can be hallucinogenic)
Panaeolina foenisecii (black or dark blackish brown spores)

Color and Description

Cap: dull cinnamon-brown or dull grayish brown with slight purplish cast when moist, fading to dingy buff with lilac tinge on drying, bell-shaped, moist but not viscid, smooth or sometimes a little wrinkled, .5–.75 inch wide; flesh pale beige, thin, fragile, with "mushroomy" odor.

Gills: pallid or brownish pallid, then dark and somewhat mottled with the spores, broad, rounded where they touch the stem.

Stem: pale toward the top, dingy brown below, very slender, rigid, fragile, hollow, smooth, longer than the width of the cap.

When and Where Found. Spring and fall, in lawns and other open grassy places, always associated with grasses. May appear in the summer on well-watered lawns.

Remarks. The haymaker's mushroom can be hallucinogenic and therefore is not recommended for the table. Along with *Marasmius oreades, Entoloma sericeum,* and *Clitocybe dealbata,* it is one of the common lawn-inhabiting mushrooms. Its brownish, bell-shaped cap, long, rigid, fragile stem, and black spores distinguish it.

Haymaker's mushroom   *Panaeolina foenisecii*

Bell-shaped panaeolus   *Panaeolus campanulatus*

BELL-SHAPED PANAEOLUS (Not recommended, possibly hallucinogenic)
Panaeolus campanulatus (black spores)

Color and Description

Cap: lead gray, gray-brown or brown, thin, bell-shaped, particles of the veil often adhering to the edge of the cap, 1–2 inches wide; flesh grayish, thin.

Gills: grayish, mottled with black spores.

Stem: gray, slender, 2–5 inches long.

When and Where Found. Spring and fall, usually on dung or in rich pasture soil.

Remarks. It is not likely that the pothunter will be tempted by this mushroom. It has been reported as possibly hallucinogenic, as have similar or related species.

RINGED PSATHYRELLA (Edibility unknown)
Psathyrella longistriata (dark purple-brown spores)

Color and Description

Cap: cone-shaped to rounded, then flattened with a broad, central knob, moist to dry, with translucent, radiating lines on the margin when moist, dark reddish brown to yellowish brown or light gray-yellow brown, fading with loss of moisture, with patches of white veil tissue often present along margin, 1–4 inches wide; flesh thin and fragile.

Gills: attached to the stem, pale buff then purplish brown.

Stem: 2–4 inches long, hollow, very fragile, white, with a wooly or fibrillose coating below the prominent, persistent, membranous, white ring left by the veil, upper surface of ring with conspicuous striations.

When and Where Found. Common in the Pacific Northwest on humus and debris; in coniferous and mixed forests, frequent where alder is found. Fruits mainly in the fall season, occasionally in the spring.

Remarks. This distinctive fungus seems restricted to the Pacific Northwest extending into California. Little is known about its edibility and therefore it is not recommended.

Ringed psathyrella   *Psathyrella longistriata*

Stuntz's psilocybe   *Psilocybe stuntzii*

STUNTZ'S PSILOCYBE (Hallucinogenic)
Psilocybe stuntzii (purple-brown spores)

Color and Description

Cap: cone-shaped to rounded or somewhat flattened, usually with a central knob, moist to sticky, with translucent radiating lines on the margin when moist, dark brown and often olive greenish on the margin, fading to yellowish brown or pale yellow on drying, 1–2 inches wide; flesh thin.

Gills: attached to the stem, off-white becoming brownish to dark brown.

Stem: 1–3 inches long, narrow, sometimes with the base enlarged, yellowish to yellow-brown or darker; the partial veil forming a fragile, membranous, bluish streaked ring which becomes a bluish or dark zone on the stem.

When and Where Found. Fruits in the fall and early winter as well as the spring seasons in the Pacific Northwest. In groups or clusters on wood chips, decayed conifer wood, also in lawns and fields. Widespread and often abundant in the Puget Sound area.

Remarks. Several blue staining, hallucinogenic psilocybes occur in the Pacific Northwest. Be very careful when identifying these species and do not confuse this group with the deadly conocybe or the deadly galerina, *Galerina venenata*.

Psilocybe semilanceata, the liberty cap, is another common hallucinogenic mushroom in the Pacific Northwest. It has a brownish, cone-shaped or bell-shaped cap with an acute knob, grayish to brownish gills, and a smooth, whitish, slender stem. There is a thin veil at first which does not leave a ring or stem. The cap margin develops bluish colors when bruised as do many species in this group. It occurs in pastures, fields and other grassy areas.

QUESTIONABLE STROPHARIA (Edible)
Stropharia ambigua (purple-brown spores)

Color and Description

Cap: clear chrome yellow, first rounded then flat, viscid when wet, margin edged with particles of white broken veil, 2–5 inches wide; flesh whitish.

Gills: white at first, then grayish, finally purple, at first concealed by white veil which, on breaking, adheres to margin of cap, forming only a slight ring on stem.

Stem: white, larger at base, lower portion covered with fluffy white scales.

When and Where Found. Fall, only occasionally in the spring, on the ground in both conifer and deciduous forests, or on their margins.

Questionable stropharia   *Stropharia ambigua*

Remarks. Although a conspicuous mushroom in the woods and easily identified, it is not a very good edible species, being flavorless or tasting of rotting leaves. A mushroom of similar appearance is *Amanita gemmata,* but the dark gills of the stropharia are quite different from the white gills of the amanita.

WINE-RED STROPHARIA (Edible)
Stropharia rugoso-annulata (grayish violet spores)

Color and Description
Cap: dull wine red or purplish red at first, finally fading to straw color, convex, dry, smooth, silky, very large, 2–8 or more inches wide; flesh white, thick, firm, no special odor.

Gills: white at first, then grayish violet, finally blackish violet with white edges, notched where they touch the stem, thin, close together.

Stem: white or pale yellowish, stout, smooth, dry; ring conspicuous, thick, with upper surface deeply radially grooved, lower part thick and feltlike, split into several radiating clawlike points that project beyond the upper part.

When and Where Found. Most often in fall, but may appear in spring or summer in areas that are frequently watered; on cultivated ground (flower beds, vegetable gardens, compost heaps, wood chips, lawns).

Remarks. Edible and choice. The wine-red cap and intricately constructed ring with its clawlike points are distinctive. Faded caps are strikingly different in color from young ones. The occurrence of this mushroom only in cultivated areas may indicate that it is not a native species. Spawn of this mushroom can be purchased and grown on wood chips and other substrates, producing a large crop of an excellent edible. Some strains of the wine-red stropharia produce extremely large fruit bodies.

Wine-red stropharia   *Stropharia rugoso-annulata*

Polypores

Polypores, like boletes, have tubes instead of gills on the undersurface of the cap. Most are stemless and grow shelflike, attached to wood by the side of the cap. Most are too tough to eat, or have a disagreeable flavor, so the group as a whole is of little interest to pothunters. A few resemble boletes, being somewhat soft and fleshy, growing on the ground, and having an umbrellalike cap and stem; these can be recognized as polypores by their light-colored spore print.

KUROTAKE (Edible)
Boletopsis leucomelaena (whitish to pale brownish spores)

Color and Description

Cap: white or very pale gray at first, soon becoming very dark brownish black, rounded, smooth, 3–6 inches wide; flesh white, thick, firm, no special odor, mild or more commonly bitter taste.

Tubes and Pores: small pores; very shallow tubes running down the stem.

Stem: white then pale gray, stout, solid, hard-fleshed, dry, dull, no longer than the width of the cap.

When and Where Found. Fall, on the ground under conifers, mostly in mountainous areas.

Remarks. Edible, but has a bitter taste that requires special treatment. The Japanese method is to soak the mushroom for a long time in brine; the bitter taste disappears, but the fungus turns black, and many Americans find that this presents a discouraging aspect for something to be eaten. *Kurotake* means "black mushroom."

Kurotake   *Boletopsis leucomelaena*

Sulfur shelf   *Laetiporus sulphureus*

SULFUR SHELF (Edible)
Laetiporus sulphureus (white spores)

Color and Description
Cap: orange to red, in wide-spreading brackets or shelves attached by the side of the cap to the tree trunk or log, almost stemless, often growing in dense series, 2–12 inches or more across, in many layers; flesh white, unchanging when bruised; strong musky odor, somewhat sour taste in age.

Tubes and Pores: clear sulphur yellow, unchanging when bruised.

Stem: slight or absent, the brackets growing directly from the host. Hundreds may grow on one log or tree.

When and Where Found. Late summer and fall, on rotting logs or stumps, occasionally from a wound in a live tree. The mycelium may live in a log for many years before fruiting bodies appear, then fruit on the same log for several seasons.

Remarks. A brilliant sight to come upon unexpectedly in the woods. When young the margin is tender and makes an excellent dish. The soft, cheesy consistency makes this polypore quite different from other bracket-shaped mushrooms seen in the woods. Other common names for *Laetiporus sulphureus* are chicken mushroom and chicken of the wood, while an earlier technical name was *Polyporus sulphureus*.

Spine Fungi

Some of the edible spine fungi grow on the ground and resemble gilled mushrooms or boletes, with umbrellalike or funnel-shaped cap and stem, but the undersurface of the cap is covered with small, downward-pointing spines instead of gills or tubes. Another type grows on wood and consists of a mass of fleshy branches ending in downward-pointing spines. The group is easily recognized and contains at least two popular edible species, as well as several that are too tough or unpleasantly flavored to eat.

The spine fungi are arranged alphabetically according to genus.

CORAL HYDNUM (Edible)
Hericium abietis (white spores)

Color and Description
Fruit Body: white or cream-white, consisting of a mass of branches coming from a common center, dividing again into branchlets which are covered with stalactite-like spines hanging from them, compact

Coral hydnum   *Hericium abietis*

when young, soon spreading into large clusters from a few inches to 2 or more feet wide and a foot or more in length as they hang from a tree or log.

Spines: white or creamy, .25–.50 inch long.

When and Where Found. Late summer through fall, in old conifer forests on fallen logs, stumps, or old trees.

Remarks. Edible and considered very good by most people. Do not eat much at one time, as the larger branches are somewhat stringy and may prove indigestible. This beautiful, impressive fungus, often very large, could not be confused with anything poisonous and so is one of the safest for the beginner to look for and try.

PECK'S HYDNUM (Inedible)
Hydnellum peckii (fawn-brown spores)

Color and Description

Cap: dark brown in the center, pale salmon pink on the margin, flat or slightly depressed in the center, surface often covered with coarse nodules, felty or woolly, exuding drops of blood-red liquid when younger in wet weather, 3–6 inches wide; flesh brown, thick, corky, fibrous, tough, with sweet odor and intensely peppery taste.

Spines: pale dingy salmon pink at first, then brown, very slender, about .25 inch long.

Stem: dark brown, felty or finely woolly, one to three inches long.

When and Where Found. Fall, on the ground under conifers, usually in dense conifer woods. Abundant in some seasons, uncommon in others.

Remarks. Inedible; the flesh is very tough and fibrous. The colors, fibrous flesh, red drops of liquid on the cap (when present), sweet odor, and very peppery taste make this an easily recognized fungus.

SPREADING-HEDGEHOG MUSHROOM (Edible)
Hydnum repandum (white spores)

Color and Description

Cap: cream, tan or reddish cinnamon, smooth or slightly scaly, first rounded then spreading and irregular, 2–4 inches wide; flesh

Peck's hydnum *Hydnellum peckii*

Spreading-hedgehog mushroom *Hydnum repandum*

white or slightly ocher, soft and brittle, taste mild or slightly bitter.

Spines: white or buff, small and somewhat fragile.

Stem: white, sometimes central but occasionally to one side of center, 2–3 inches long.

When and Where Found. Fall, on the ground, in coniferous forests; frequently found at low elevations in the Olympic and Cascade mountains.

Remarks. A good edible mushroom, considered by some as good as the chanterelle. It resembles the chanterelle in appearance, but the spines on the lower surface make it unmistakable. *Hydnum umbilicatum* is smaller, more slender, and has a sunken cap center.

SCALY HYDNUM (Edible with caution)
Sarcodon imbricatum (dull brown spores)

Color and Description

Cap: dull brown with purplish tinge, the scales often darker, convex then flattened and somewhat sunken in the center, covered with coarse scales with free tips, 3–6 inches wide; flesh pale grayish buff, thick, pale, mild taste or slight taste of fresh meal.

Spines: pale grayish brown with lilac tinge, becoming darker brown, pointed, soft, sometimes running down the stem slightly, about .25 to .5 inch long.

Stem: pale grayish buff, sometimes more brownish, stout, tapering at the base, shorter than the width of the cap.

When and Where Found. Fall, on the ground in conifer woods.

Remarks. Edible, but should be tried cautiously, as some persons are made ill by it. Only young and mild specimens should be used. A similar species, the rough-capped hydnum (*Sarcodon scabrosum*), has a blackish green stem base and a very bitter taste. It is not edible.

Scaly hydnum   *Sarcodon imbricatum*

Coral Fungi

The mushrooms in this group consist of erect, simple, cylindrical to club-shaped or large, fleshy, branched fruit bodies, hence the popular name "coral." Avoid those in which the flesh in the base of the plant is rubbery and translucent, like stiff gelatin, and those that have a disagreeable taste when fresh or after cooking. If these precautions are observed, various corals can be sampled with little fear—subject, of course, to the standard rule of always trying any new mushroom in small quantity for the first time.

The corals are arranged alphabetically according to genus, and alphabetically by species within each genus.

PURPLE CLUB CORAL (Edible)
Clavaria purpurea (white spores)

Color and Description

Fruit Body: purple to grayish purple or brownish gray-purple, cylindrical to spindle-shaped, simple, 1–5 inches tall, up to .25 inch thick, fragile, base white and hairy; flesh whitish to purplish, brittle.

When and Where Found. Common in the Pacific Northwest, during the summer and fall seasons. In clusters, on the ground in conifer or mixed woods, at times locally abundant, for example, on mossy road banks.

Remarks. The purple club coral is one of our most striking fall species. The white worm coral, *Clavaria vermicularis,* produces white worm-like clubs. Both are edible but probably not commonly collected for food because of fragile nature and lack of substance of their fruit bodies.

FLAT-TOPPED CORAL (Edible)
Clavariadelphus truncatus (pale yellowish spores)

Color and Description

Fruit Body: pinkish brown to yellowish ochre or orange, the top

Purple club coral *Clavaria purpurea*

Flat-topped coral *Clavariadelphus truncatus*

usually more orange or yellow than the sides, club-shaped with a flattened or shallowly depressed top, the sides with shallow wrinkles, simple or rarely forked, 2–6 inches tall, 1–3.5 inches wide; base paler to whitish; flesh whitish to ochre, firm to spongy, taste sweet to bland.

When and Where Found. Scattered or in groups or small clusters, on the ground under conifers, late summer and fall seasons.

Remarks. Two nearly identical species occur in North America, *Clavariadelphus truncatus* and *Clavariadelphus borealis;* the latter differs from the former mainly by its white spores. Both are edible but apparently not of high quality. *Clavariadelphus pistillaris* is a similar species that is club-shaped and has a bitter taste.

CRESTED CORAL (Edible)
Clavulina cristata (white spores)

Color and Description
Fruit Body: white, dingy ivory, pale gray, or tinged with violet, many slender branches from a stemlike base, the branches toothed or crested at their tips, often irregular and somewhat flattened, 3–4 inches tall, mild taste and odor.

When and Where Found. Fall, on the ground in conifer woods.

Remarks. Edible and considered excellent by many. One of the Pacific Northwest's commonest coral fungi, often making up in numbers what it lacks in size. The gray form and the purplish or lavender form are sometimes given separate names, but the colors seem to overlap so it is hard to make distinctions based on color alone.

Crested coral   *Clavulina cristata*

This coral is often parasitized by another fungus that turns it black and makes it thicker and knobby. These parasitized specimens should be discarded when collecting for the table.

BLAH CORAL (Poisonous)
Ramaria acrisiccescens (yellowish spores)

Color and Description
Fruit Body: branches pale yellow-brown to pale orange-brown with pallid or faintly pinkish to purplish tinted tips, base white, base and lower branches bruising brown, 2–12 inches tall, 2–6 inches wide; branches subparallel, elongated, tips rounded; flesh brownish white, fleshy to stringy; taste mild to acid when fresh, stronger when cooked.

When and Where Found. On the ground in mixed, old conifer forests in the fall season.

Remarks. This is a common fall coral in the Pacific Northwest, but is one of several in a closely related group. They have in common pallid, yellowish or brownish fruit bodies, sometimes with the tips flushed pink or lavender, elongate, nearly parallel ascending branches, and a bitter-acid taste when fresh, cooked, or dried. As a group they are considered poisonous and should be avoided.

Blah coral *Ramaria acrisiccescens*

Carmine coral *Ramaria araiospora*

CARMINE CORAL (Edible)
Ramaria araiospora (yellowish spores)

Color and Description

Fruit Body: branches vivid red when young, fading in age, tips becoming yellowish, base white to pale yellow, sometimes discoloring to pale brown, 2–5.5 inches tall, 1–3.5 inches wide; branches somewhat divergent, elongating in age, tips rounded to sharply pointed; flesh same color as surface, fleshy to stringy; mild taste.

When and Where Found. On the ground under western hemlock, fruiting in the fall season.

Remarks. This beautiful coral comes in two forms, the one described above and var. *rubella,* which is more magenta red in color and does not develop yellow on the branch tips in age. Both are edible. In the past this coral was confused with *Ramaria subbotrytis,* the rose coral. Other similar corals are *Ramaria stuntzii,* which is robust, scarlet at first then orangish red, with the base white; and *Ramaria cyaneigranosa,* another large species which is light red to pink with a white base and sometimes yellow tips. Both are reported as edible. *Ramaria rubripermanens,* a choice edible spring coral of the Inland Empire, has pale branches and light dull "red wine" shaded tips when mature. It is large, has a white, massive base, and the tips of the branches are dark reddish brown when young and fresh. It is similar in appearance to the wine-tipped coral, *Ramaria botrytis*.

FUZZY-FOOTED CORAL (Edibility unknown)
Ramaria cystidiophora (yellowish spores)

Color and Description
Fruit Body: lower branches light buff yellow with ultimate branches and tips light yellow, the base pale yellow to white and covered with a white cottony fuzz, 4–5 inches tall; branches slender, tips sharp pointed; base long, single or in a fused or tufted structure; flesh cartilaginous, somewhat fragile; odor anise-like (licorice).

When and Where Found. On the ground in deep humus beneath stands of Douglas fir, western hemlock and western red cedar in the fall.

Remarks. The fuzzy-footed coral is characterized by clear, bright yellow fruit bodies when in prime condition. There are several variations, all tending to produce a somewhat fused or tufted base with a pronounced covering of white cottony fuzz. The edibility of the species is unknown.

Fuzzy-footed coral   *Ramaria cystidiophora*

Orange jelly-belly coral   *Ramaria gelatiniaurantia*

ORANGE JELLY-BELLY CORAL (Edibility unknown, caution advised)

Ramaria gelatiniaurantia (yellowish spores)

Color and Description

Fruit Body: upper branches and tips deep orange, just above ground level light to bright yellow, the base white where underground, 2–9 inches tall, 2–5 inches wide, cluster-like, lower branches sometimes fused, base consisting of many fused gelatinous "stems," tips pointed; flesh yellowish in tips, marbled with clear and whitish streaks in base, texture gelatinous; taste mild, odor bean-like.

When and Where Found. On the ground in coniferous woods containing western hemlock. Fruits in the fall season.

Remarks. The edibility of this orange coral is apparently unknown. However, its gelatinous consistency indicates that it could be toxic to some individuals. Another common orange coral is *Ramaria sandaracina*. The color is similar to *Ramaria gelatiniaurantia* and the flesh in the base is somewhat gelatinous, indicating that it could be toxic. It turns grayish violet where bruised. Also compare the Oregon gelatinous coral.

OREGON GELATINOUS CORAL (Poisonous)
Ramaria gelatinosa var. *oregonensis* (yellowish spores)

Color and Description
Fruit Bodies: branches light orange but becoming darker and duller with age, developing grayish and brownish tones, sometimes with a violet gray cast, tips same colored as branches or paler, base white, light yellow or light orange, 3–6 inches tall, 2–5 inches wide; base broad, fused, covered with white fuzz; branches nearly parallel with rounded tips; flesh pale dull orange, translucent, in base like stiff gelatin; taste mild, odor musty sweet.

When and Where Found. On the ground in old coniferous forests, often under western hemlock. Fruiting in the fall season.

Remarks. This is among the most "gelatinous" of the corals in the Pacific Northwest. It seems to cause gastrointestinal poisoning consistently and should not be eaten. Compare the orange jelly-belly, which also has a gelatinous interior.

Oregon gelatinous coral   *Ramaria gelatinosa* var. *oregonensis*

Northwest spring coral   *Ramaria rasilispora*

NORTHWEST SPRING CORAL (Edible with caution)
Ramaria rasilispora (yellowish spores)

Color and Description

Fruit Body: branches and tips pale dull orange-yellow to deeper orange-yellow then pale dull orange when mature, the tips dark brown with age, base off-white, 2–6 inches tall, about the same width, cauliflower-like for a long time; base stout, lower branches thick, tips rounded; flesh white, texture fleshy and stringy to soft fibrous; taste not distinctive.

When and Where Found. On the ground in coniferous woods, usually where true fir occurs. Fruiting in the spring and summer.

Remarks. This is one of the common spring corals. Another very large coral, *Ramaria magnipes,* occurs in the late spring and early summer in large quantities in the Inland Empire. It is distinguished from *R. rasilispora* by its more intensely yellow fruiting bodies, more massive base, and bitterness when cooked. Both are collected for food in large quantities, but some people are adversely affected by them, suffering gastrointestinal upset. So try them with caution and cook all specimens thoroughly.

CAULIFLOWER MUSHROOM (Edible)
Sparassis crispa (white spores)

Color and Description
Fruit Body: cream-white mass consisting of ribbonlike branches arising from a single, long, pointed base, 6 inches to 3 feet wide, weight up to forty pounds; texture firm, pleasant odor.

When and Where Found. Fall, in conifer forests, base often attached to the root of a tree.

Remarks. This large, remarkable-looking mushroom growth is one of the best of the edible species. Cut the mushroom off at ground level; do not pull it up. Cauliflower mushrooms will fruit for several years from the same base if the base is left in the ground. In the past the western cauliflower mushroom was called *Sparassis radicata*.

Cauliflower mushroom   *Sparassis crispa*

Jelly Fungi

These curious mushrooms have, as their name suggests, a consistency like rubbery gelatin, or sometimes very soft gelatin. They adorn our forests with a variety of colors and interesting forms, but do not have much to offer to the mushroom eater. None is known to be poisonous, but they have little or no flavor and their peculiar texture does not appeal to everyone. If cooked, they usually melt, leaving only thin membranes, so one must eat them raw, pickled, or marinated. The genera and species are presented in alphabetical order.

TREE-EAR (Edible)
Auricularia auricula (white spores)

Color and Description
Fruit body: cuplike to ear-shaped, 1–6 inches wide, upper surface smooth, wavy, dark brown to reddish brown or blackish; undersurface covered with dense, minute hairs, irregularly ribbed and veined, reddish brown to yellowish brown; flesh thin, rubbery.

When and Where Found. Scattered or clustered on conifer logs, often fir; common in the western mountains in the summer, fall and winter, usually most prevalent after heavy rains. Fruit bodies typically occur on conifer logs with the bark still on them.

Remarks. This large jelly fungus, known as the tree-ear or wood-ear, is related to *Auricularia polytricha,* Ho-Elor, which is grown commercially in China and other regions of the Orient. Although the tree-ear looks similar to some of the large cup fungi, the latter are typically more fragile and grow on the ground or on rotten wood.

ORANGE JELLY (Edible)
Dacrymyces palmatus (orange-yellow spores)

Color and Description
Fruit Body: Growing from wood as a bright orange, lobed, irregular mass half an inch to 1 or 2 inches wide; firm and rubbery at first,

Tree-ear   *Auricularia auricula*

Orange jelly   *Dacrymyces palmatus*

but soon becoming soft, and often melting into a soupy mass when old.

When and Where Found. Late fall, sometimes continuing into winter if the weather is not too severe; on wood, in practically any kind of forest.

Remarks. This is one of the Pacific Northwest's commonest jelly fungi, usually not appearing in abundance until the weather has become decidedly cool, in late fall. The fruiting bodies might make a colorful addition to a green salad, but otherwise have little appeal to the palate. Only young specimens are firm enough to be considered for eating.

APRICOT JELLY MUSHROOM (Edible)
Phlogiotis helvelloides (white spores)

Color and Description

Fruit Body: apricot or salmon color, often fading to pale orange, gelatinous, somewhat funnel-shaped or like a little calla lily, surface smooth, 1–3 inches tall.

Apricot jelly mushroom   *Phlogiotis helvelloides*

When and Where Found. Late summer and fall, in damp ground on rotting wood, often under Douglas firs.

Remarks. May be pickled in vinegar, candied in sugar syrup, or eaten raw in salad.

WHITE JELLY MUSHROOM (Edible)
Pseudohydnum gelatinosum

Color and Description

Cap: translucent white, sometimes shaded gray, gelatinous, erect on twigs or attached by the side on decaying logs, minute spines on the undersurface or spore-bearing surface, 1–3 inches in height or width.

When and Where Found. Fall after heavy rains, in Douglas fir forests.

Remarks. A very beautiful little mushroom. It is of slight value as food, but may be eaten raw with sugar and cream, or marinated in french dressing and used in salad.

White jelly mushroom *Pseudohydnum gelatinosum*

WITCH'S BUTTER (Edible)
Tremella lutescens (yellowish spores)

Color and Description
Growing from wood as a yellow to orange-yellow, irregularly lobed or brainlike, tough gelatinous mass, 1–4 inches wide, orange-red and horny when dried.

When and Where Found. Throughout the year depending on location and weather conditions; widespread on wood of hardwood trees.

Remarks. The jelly fungi in this group are considered tasteless and inedible by many individuals. They can be added to soups and other dishes, however. Compare it with the orange jelly. Witch's butter has also been called *Tremella mesenterica*.

Witch's butter   *Tremella lutescens*

Puffballs, Earthstars, and False Truffles

These types of mushrooms can be easily recognized by the beginner. There are several types, most of which are safe and good to eat, if certain precautions are observed. All the thick-skinned puffballs, the genus *Scleroderma,* are poisonous. Always cut puffballs in half lengthwise and look for any signs of gills being formed, which would indicate that you have the "button stage" of a gilled mushroom, possibly a poisonous amanita. Also make sure that the interior tissue is uniformly white, discarding any with even a slight tinge of yellow. This discoloration means that the tissue has begun to decompose and will be altered in flavor and may cause illness if eaten.

TUMBLING PUFFBALL (Edible)
Bovista pila (purplish brown spores)

Color and Description
Fruit Body: 1–3.5 inches wide, round or nearly so, attached to the ground by a small cord which breaks at maturity, outer surface white or slightly pinkish, flaking off at maturity and exposing a thin, tough, persistent, shiny bronze or coppery metallic inner spore case which cracks open at the top; interior white at first, then brown to purplish brown at maturity.

When and Where Found. Summer and fall, widespread; single or in groups, in grassy areas, stables, corrals, or open woods.

Remarks. This puffball commonly becomes detached and is blown about, dumping spores as it tumbles along. Often the old spore cases overwinter. The lead colored puffball, *Bovista plumbea,* is similar but somewhat smaller in size and attached to the soil by a small patch of fibers rather than a small cord. Its white outer layer peels off in sheets, exposing a bluish gray to purplish umber persistent spore case. Both of these bovistas are good edibles when the interior is still white.

Tumbling puffball *Bovista pila*

WARTED GIANT PUFFBALL (Edible)
Calbovista subsculpta (yellow-brown to olive-brown spores)

Color and Description
Fruit Body: white, pear-shaped or spherical, about 3–6 inches in diameter; outer surface at first cracked into large, coarse warts—like pyramids with their tops cut off, about half an inch wide at their bases and nearly as high; flesh firm, white, turning yellow then dark olive-brown as the spores mature.

When and Where Found. Spring or fall, on the ground under conifers in the mountains, often found under ponderosa pine on the eastern slope of the Cascade Mountains.

Remarks. Edible, and much sought after in some parts of the Pacific Northwest. Its coarsely warted outer surface easily distinguishes it from the giant puffball, but not so readily from the Sierran puffball, which also is coarsely warted. There the distinction is a microscopic one, having to do with the thread-like material (capillitium) among which the spores are found.

BOONE'S GIANT PUFFBALL (Edible)
Calvatia booniana (olive-brown spores)

Color and Description
Fruit Body: very large, 8–24 inches wide, round but usually

Warted giant puffball   *Calbovista subsculpta*

Boone's giant puffball   *Calvatia booniana*

flattened or compressed somewhat, with a rootlike attachment at the
base; outer surface buff or pale brownish, composed of large flat warts
or scales and breaking into polygonal plates which fall away as the
spores mature; interior white, gradually yellowish, then olive-brown
when the spore mass ripens.

When and Where Found. Following summer rains, on soil under sagebrush and juniper and in arid areas of the west.

Remarks. Like other true puffballs this is a fine edible. Eat it— and other true puffballs—when the interior is white; a tinge of yellow often means a bitter taste. *Calvatia booniana* is also known as the western giant puffball. Its close relative, *Calvatia gigantea,* the giant puffball, is similar in size and shape but the surface is smooth, like fine kid leather, before breaking into flat plates. It occurs in brushy areas, woods, pastures and occasionally in urban surroundings during the late spring, summer, or fall. In recent literature both of these species have been classified in the genus *Langermannia*.

SIERRAN PUFFBALL (Edible)
Calvatia sculpta (yellow-brown spores)

Color and Description

Fruit Body: white, pear-shaped, 2–4 inches wide, covered with long, sharp-pointed, narrowly pyramidal warts up to 1 inch long; one to several warts arise from angular plaques into which the outer wall has cracked and which fall away one by one, revealing the dusty mass of spores; flesh firm and white at first, turning yellow to olive-brown.

When and Where Found. Summer or early fall, under conifers at high elevations in the mountains of the West Coast.

Remarks. This spectacular spiny puffball is usually found by people exploring mountain trails at higher elevations. It looks something like the warted giant puffball, but its spines are much longer and sharper. The most reliable difference between them is a microscopic one (see the remarks under *Calbovista subsculpta*).

Sierran puffball *Calvatia sculpta*

Rounded earthstar *Geastrum saccatum*

ROUNDED EARTHSTAR (Inedible)
Geastrum saccatum (brown to purplish brown spores)

Color and Description
Fruit Body: when open, a roundish, non-stalked spore sac in a bowl-like depression of starlike rays that curve back on themselves, up to 2 inches wide; spore sac papery, unpolished, purplish drab to dull brown, with a small, central, circular depression around a raised mouth-like opening; starlike rays pale to brownish on the upper (inner) surface, outer surface yellowish buff to brownish; interior white and firm, forming a brown to purplish brown, powdery spore mass at maturity. When unopened resembling a small puffball; a thickish outer layer and interior spore sac are seen when cut in half.

When and Where Found. Summer and fall. Widespread, often several to many in one area, usually in all stages of development. In leaf litter, rich humus, around old stumps.

Remarks. Several earthstars occur in the Pacific Northwest, *Geastrum saccatum* being one of the more common ones. All are considered inedible because of their texture.

Gem-studded puffball   *Lycoperdon |perlatum*

GEM-STUDDED PUFFBALL (Edible)
Lycoperdon perlatum (olive-brown spores)

Color and Description

Fruit Body: white or pale dingy cream or pale dingy brownish, somewhat pear-shaped, about 3–4 inches tall, 1–2 inches wide above, at maturity with a pore at the top through which the spores escape, often with a rather long, stemlike base, covered all over with small, short, conical or pyramidal spines that break off easily leaving a smooth spot; flesh white, then greenish yellow, then olive-brown.

When and Where Found. Fall, in woods of various kinds, also in lawns or on cultivated ground.

Remarks. Edible and of good quality as long as the flesh is pure white. This is one of the Pacific Northwest's commonest puffballs, easily recognized by its long stem base and small, short spines that fall off.

PEAR-SHAPPED PUFFBALL (Edible)
Lycoperdon pyriforme (olive-brown spores)

Color and Description

Fruit Body: some shade of brown on the upper portion, white at the

Pear-shaped puffball   *Lycoperdon pyriforme*

base, which is fastened to white, stringlike strands of mycelium; about 2–2.5 inches tall, 1 inch wide at the top, covered with small warts and granules making the surface rough; flesh white, then greenish yellow, finally olive brown.

When and Where Found. Fall, in dense, compact clusters, often of dozens of individuals, on rotten wood or at the base of stumps, in conifer or mixed forests.

Remarks. Edible and choice if young and firm and flesh is pure white. The crowded clusters of brown, pear-shaped puffballs make this species easy to recognize.

WESTERN RHIZOPOGON (Not recommended)
Rhizopogon occidentalis (yellow-brown spore mass)

Color and Description

Fruit Body: nearly round to irregularly shaped, somewhat potato-like, totally or partially underground, .5–2.5 inches wide; surface white when young, becoming bright yellow with greenish tint, often developing some brownish to reddish areas but not rapidly staining when injured or cut, coated with small fibrils and more conspicuous buff to brownish or reddish brown chord-like strands; interior firm,

Western rhizopogon   *Rhizopogon occidentalis*

pallid to pale greenish gray, drying grayish yellow to yellow-brown; odor may be fruity in older specimens.

When and Where Found. Fruiting in the fall season, solitary or in groups, often in sandy soil. Occurs under conifers, especially under lodgepole pine, and seems to be most common in the coastal region.

Remarks. The western rhizopogon is one of many species in the Pacific Northwest. All of them fruit totally or partially buried in the soil or humus and commonly are called "false truffles." They are often dug up and eaten by rodents, deer, and other animals and probably are edible. However, since we know little about their edibility, and because the genus itself, as well as the species, are difficult to identify, they are not recommended for eating.

Other common rhizopogons are *R. parksii* and *R. ellenae.* The former is widespread and usually found at low elevations in coniferous forests, particularly with Douglas fir and western hemlock. The surface of the fruit body is pallid with an overlay of small dark brown to purple-black fibrils at first, and then becomes dark brown to purple-black overall. When bruised the fruiting body quickly stains blue or blue-violet and then blackish. The latter is large, and the surface is white or whitish, often developing brownish or blackish areas in age. There is no rapid color change when bruised, but cut or broken surfaces may turn reddish after several minutes of exposure. It is most frequently found under ponderosa pine.

THICK-SKINNED PUFFBALL (Poisonous)
Scleroderma citrinum (blackish brown or blackish violet spores)

Color and Description

Fruit Body: dingy yellowish or dingy brown, with white, stringlike strands of mycelium attached to the base, spherical, sometimes lobed or irregular, surface smooth or cracked into small, irregular plaques; the "rind" or spore case thick, hard, finally cracking open in an irregular manner; flesh firm, hard, not spongy, white in very young specimens, but soon turning grayish violet then blackish violet, sometimes somewhat mottled, eventually becoming a violet-black or blackish brown powder.

When and Where Found. Fall, sometimes also in spring, on the ground or sometimes partly buried, in woods, along paths, also in gardens, flower beds, or under cultivated shrubs.

Remarks. Avoid sclerodermas; most persons are made ill by them. The several *Scleroderma* species of the Pacific Northwest are not well understood, but they have some common features that make them fairly easy to recognize: the thick, hard, persistent rind or outer wall, and the purplish color assumed by the flesh at an early stage. The flesh is hard and solid, not spongy like that of the lycoperdons or calvatias, and looks mottled when the purple color develops. Most sclerodermas have a disagreeable taste and somewhat pungent odor.

Thick-skinned puffball   *Scleroderma citrinum*

Cup Fungi, Helvellas, Morels, False Morels, and Truffles

In this type of mushroom the spores are produced in a tiny, club-shaped cell, the ascus (plural, asci), and are shot out with considerable force when mature. Hundreds of thousands of these tiny asci packed closely together make up the spore-bearing surface of a cup fungus of ordinary size. When a mature cup is picked, a slight jar or a slight change in humidity may cause several thousand asci to discharge their spores at the same time, like a little cloud of steam rising from the cup. You may even hear a faint hissing sound when the "puffing" takes place.

As with other groups of mushrooms, different people may have different reactions to the same species within this group, hence an unfamiliar species should be tried in *small quantity* the first time. Several of these fungi contain toxins that are broken down by heat, so

Orange fairy cup   *Aleuria aurantia*

they are safe when cooked thoroughly. From this it follows that cup fungi and their allies should not be eaten raw. Read the section on gyromitrins in the chapter on mushroom poisons before eating these fungi.

Genera and species are presented in alphabetical order.

ORANGE FAIRY CUP (Edible)
Aleuria aurantia (whitish spores)

Color and Description
Fruit Body: Inner surface brilliant orange to orange-yellow, outer surface whitish or orange-yellow, cup-shaped to saucer-shaped, .75 inch to 4 inches wide, growing scattered or clustered.

When and Where Found. In the fall, less abundantly in spring; on the ground, in the open, often along newly graded roads or along logging roads.

Remarks. Edible and pleasant-tasting. Although there is very little substance to the cups, the quantity in which these orange cups can be gathered may make them worthwhile.

BLUE-STAINING CUP (Poisonous)
Caloscypha fulgens (whitish spores)

Color and Description
Fruit Body: irregularly cup-shaped, often lopsided, up to 2 inches wide, inner surface bright orange or yellow and often with blue-green or olive-green stains, outer surface olive to blue or greenish blue; flesh brittle; solitary, scattered or in clusters.

When and Where Found. During the spring and early summer, in boggy places or in mountain coniferous forests. Often on soil and duff shortly after the snow recedes in the Pacific Northwest and Rocky Mountains.

Remarks. *Caloscypha fulgens* can be extremely abundant near the edges of snowbanks in the Cascades in some years. It is most easily confused with the edible *Aleuria aurantia,* which is brighter orange and does not stain olive or greenish. It is known that *Caloscypha fulgens* in the Pacific Northwest is poisonous, at least to some individuals.

Blue-staining cup   *Caloscypha fulgens*

PIG'S EAR (Edible with caution)
Discina perlata (whitish spores)

Color and Description
Fruit Body: cup-shaped to disc-shaped, expanding, often sunken in
the center and the surface wrinkled or convoluted, sometimes with a
short stem, inner surface tan, yellow-brown, or darker brown, outer
surface pale to whitish, 2–4 inches wide; flesh brittle; scattered to
clustered.

When and Where Found. Fruits in the spring and may be one of
the "snowbank fungi" in the western mountains. Common, widespread in conifer forests; on soil, duff or rotting wood.

Remarks. *Discina perlata* is one of several species of this genus in
western North America. Though the genus is listed as edible in some
references, it should be eaten with caution, if at all, since the species
are related to the false morels, gyromitras, some of which are poisonous.

Pig's ear *Discina perlata*

CALIFORNIA ELFIN SADDLE (Edible but not recommended)
Gyromitra californica (whitish spores)

Color and Description

Cap: tan to olive-brown in undulating folds, sometimes saddle-shaped, at other times broad and rounded, edge inrolled, white beneath, 2–4 inches wide.

Stem: white, fluted in wide, flat folds, 3–4 inches long, stained rose at the base.

When and Where Found. Usually in light soil in conifer woods, along old logging roads, moist banks along trails and other open areas in the woods.

Remarks. Little is known of the edibility of this species, so it cannot be recommended. If you insist on eating it, try a small quantity the first time. Never eat it raw; parboil it and discard the water. Never eat it in large quantities or at several successive meals. Similar species are hooded helvella, brain mushroom, and giant

California elfin saddle *Gyromitra californica*

helvella. The flanged, white stem with rose-colored base and the thin, membranous brown cap are the features that characterize the California elfin saddle.

BRAIN MUSHROOM (Poisonous)
Gyromitra esculenta (yellowish spores)

Color and Description

Cap: brown to dark reddish-brown, rounded to saddle-shaped, irregular, wrinkled or folded into many convolutions (like the lobes of the brain), not pitted with distinct depressions as is the morel, 3–4 inches wide.

Stem: white or brownish, the cap attached near the top, smooth, often grooved, hollow or with one to two chambers, 2–3 inches long.

When and Where Found. Spring and summer, on the ground under various types of trees, particularly conifers, or in the open at the edges of woods.

Remarks. The brain mushroom has several other common names:

Brain mushroom   *Gyromitra esculenta*

beefsteak morel, lorchel, edible fake morel, false morel, and conifer false morel. It also has had the scientific name *Helvella esculenta*. The species name *esculenta* means "edible," but this is hardly the case. It can cause acute illness and has caused deaths in eastern North America and Europe. Poisonings by it are not common in western North America and therefore it has in the past been recommended as an edible in the Pacific Northwest. However, this can no longer be done in view of our present understanding of its toxins. See the section on gyromitrins in the chapter on mushroom poisons for further details.

If you still insist on eating *Gyromitra esculenta*, follow these precautions: before cooking, parboil the fruit bodies and discard the water at least twice, rinsing thoroughly after each boiling; never eat large quantities of the brain mushroom; do not eat it several days in succession.

Giant helvella *Gyromitra gigas*

GIANT HELVELLA (Edible with caution)
Gyromitra gigas (whitish spores)

Color and Description
Cap: ocher yellow or tan to darker brown, wrinkled or folded into many convolutions, 4–9 inches wide; flesh solid, brittle.

Stem: white, ridged and folded lengthwise, with multiple channels within, nearly as thick as the cap, often nearly or quite hidden by the margin of the cap which comes down over it almost to the ground.

When and Where Found. Spring, or early summer, on the ground under conifers, often near melting snowfields, hence sometimes called the snowbank false morel or snow morel.

Remarks. Edible, and considered excellent by most people. Care should be taken to distinguish it from the brain mushroom and the hooded helvella. In cooking the giant helvella, first parboil, throw away the water, rinse the pieces, then proceed with the cooking. Eat only a small quantity on first trial. Do not eat large quantities or several meals in succession. Some of the recent literature refers to the western form of this mushroom as *Gyromitra montana*. In older literature it was called *Helvella gigas*.

HOODED HELVELLA (Poisonous)
Gyromitra infula (whitish spores)

Color and Description

Cap: cinnamon or dark brown, thin skin folded into a saddle shape, 2–3 inches wide.

Stem: light purplish brown, usually smooth, sometimes grooved or folded.

When and Where Found. Late summer and fall, occasionally in the spring, on rotten wood or on old logs in the forest.

Remarks. The hooded helvella, like the brain mushroom, is poisonous and should not be eaten. Its close relative *Gyromitra ambigua* is also poisonous. See remarks under brain mushroom.

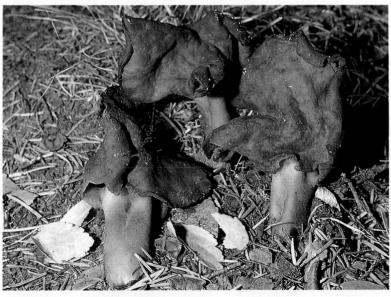

Hooded helvella   *Gyromitra infula*

ELFIN SADDLE (Edible with caution)
Helvella lacunosa (whitish spores)

Color and Description
Cap: white, gray, or black, somewhat wrinkled, cone-shaped to saddle-shaped, 1–3 inches wide; flesh thin, brittle.

Stem: white or shaded gray, grooved with conspicuous longitudinal depressions, typically 2–4 inches long.

When and Where Found. Fall after heavy rains, on the ground in Douglas fir forests, or in older thickets, or along the margins of patches of bracken.

Remarks. Although the flavor is similar to that of the morel, great care should be taken in testing this mushroom. Gather only fresh, young specimens, as old specimens develop poisonous characteristics. They should never be tasted raw and should be blanched in boiling water before cooking. Try a small quantity before eating larger amounts. Do not eat large quantities at one time and do not eat it several days in succession.

Elfin saddle   *Helvella lacunosa*

Lobster mushroom   *Hypomyces lactifluorum*

LOBSTER MUSHROOM (Edible with caution)
Hypomyces lactifluorum (spore color not applicable)

Color and Description

Not a mushroom, but a parasitic mold which grows on mushrooms of the genera *Russula* or *Lactarius*. The mushroom appears aborted and malformed and has an orange to orange-red or reddish purple covering over its surface. The surface of the mushroom, especially where the gills would have normally formed, becomes bumpy when the mold produces tiny flask-like vessels in which pale spores are produced.

When and Where Found. Summer and fall, depending on the season. Widespread and at times common in conifer and hardwood forests.

Remarks. This fungus parasite, a mold or ascomycete, often transforms its host, a *Russula* or *Lactarius*, into an excellent edible. However, one must be aware of the potential for being poisoned. What if the host mushroom happens to be poisonous? Since the host mushroom often cannot be identified once parasitized, don't eat this fungus unless you can identify the host mushroom and know that it is edible.

Black morel   *Morchella elata*

BLACK MOREL (Edible)
Morchella elata (yellowish spores)

Color and Description

Cap: pits yellow-brown or soon darker, ridges smoky, dark gray or blackish, often blackish overall at maturity, cone-shaped to more rounded in shape, normally with a rounded top, hollow, fastened by the lower edge to the stem or the edge slightly free, ridges aligned lengthwise and connected by cross ridges, often forming distinctly elongate pits, generally 1–2 inches long, up to 2 inches wide, typically wider than the diameter of the stem.

Stem: whitish to cream, hollow, roughened to granular overall, up to 5 inches long.

When and Where Found. Fruits during the spring and summer, depending on elevation, rarely fruiting in the fall. Often occurring in large numbers in spring the year following a forest fire. Found in coniferous and hardwood forests, orchards, and in gardens and similar places, particularly where bark or woody mulch have been applied.

Remarks. *Morchella elata* has been called *Morchella conica;* further study is needed to determine if they are one and the same species. Certainly they are similar to *Morchella angusticeps*. The latter has a narrow, cone-shaped, grayish cap that is blacker in age, especially on the ridges, and the stem is about as wide as the cap. In addition, large forms of *Morchella elata* attain the size of *Morchella crassipes* and certain forms with a nearly half-free cap resemble *Morchella semilibera*. The latter species also occurs here but is not as common as the black morels. See comments under *Verpa bohemica*.

The black morels are often found in quantity under conifers and their understory shrubs along the eastern slopes of the Cascade Mountains. The experienced morel hunter always searches very carefully those areas where a forest fire has occurred the preceeding summer, as various black morels are often found there in abundance the first year, less the second year, and still less or not at all thereafter.

The black morels are considered edible but certain individuals get gastrointestinal upset from eating them, so they should be eaten cautiously the first time. Eat only clean specimens, free of decay. Cook all morels, as well as other mushrooms, thoroughly. In the case of morels, and certain other mushrooms, consumption of alcoholic beverages along with the meal may be related to ill effects.

EDIBLE MOREL (Edible)
Morchella esculenta (yellowish spores)

Color and Description

Cap: pale brownish cream, yellow to tan or pale brown to grayish brown, edges of the ridges usually not darker than the pits, oval in outline, sometimes bluntly cone-shaped with a rounded top or more elongate, hollow, fastened to the stem at its lower edge, covered with rather deep pits, the ridges between pits running irregularly in all directions, typically about 2–4 inches long and half as wide.

Stem: white to pallid or pale yellow, hollow, straight or having a club-shaped or bulbous base, finely granular overall, somewhat ridged, generally about 2–3 inches long and 1–1.5 inches thick.

When and Where Found. April, May, and sometimes June, in various forests, orchards, yards, gardens and sometimes in recently burned areas.

Remarks. *Morchella esculenta* appears to be a variable species and has a variety of interpretations in the literature. It is, however, distinctive from the black morels and fruits a little later or at about the same time as them. In the west it does not appear to be as common as *Morchella elata* and its relatives. However, it can be locally abundant. *Morchella crassipes* appears to be a very large version of *Morchella esculenta,* with a larger and often more elongate cap and usually an enlarged stem base. There is another morel with pale, whitish to grayish or grayish brown ridges and contrasting dark gray to gray-brown or blackish, deep pits, also found in western North America. This has been called the white morel, *Morchella deliciosa;* however, the correct name for it remains unclear.

Morchella esculenta and its relatives, like all morels, are among the most highly prized of all edible fungi. It is well documented, however, that some individuals have a bad reaction to morels, so if you have never eaten morels before try them cautiously at first. Confusion over the names for the various varieties and forms of the edible morels calls for extensive careful study. For the mushroom hunter, however, distinctions between the various species of morels is academic, all species being equally edible and considered delicious.

Edible morel   *Morchella esculenta*

The spreading peziza   *Peziza repanda*

THE SPREADING PEZIZA (Edibility unknown)
Peziza repanda (whitish spores)

Color and Description

Fruit Body: cup-shaped to saucer-shaped, then spreading to flat, up to 5 inches wide, inner surface tan to brown, outer surface whitish; flesh brittle.

When and Where Found. Spring, summer and fall or in the winter in warmer regions; common and widespread throughout forested areas as well as in gardens; scattered or clustered on rotten wood, duff or soil.

Remarks. *Peziza repanda* is one of many species of *Peziza* in North America and merely serves here as an example of this common group. *Peziza badia* and its relatives are darker brown or more reddish brown than *P. repanda*. Other species, such as *Peziza praetivisa*, are purple in color; *Peziza praetivisa* occurs on burned areas. The edibility of pezizas is unknown. They are not recommended as food.

Violet star cup   *Sarcosphaera crassa*

VIOLET STAR CUP (Not recommended)
Sarcosphaera crassa (pale yellowish spores)

Color and Description

Cup: Growing as a hollow sphere, 2–4 inches in diameter, just below the surface of the ground, then barely breaking the surface and splitting into pointed segments that open out starlike; outer surface white, but usually dingy from adhering soil, inner spore-bearing surface white or pale at first, then a beautiful shade of violet.

When and Where Found. Spring through summer, infrequently in the fall, on the ground in sandy or soft soil. In the Pacific Northwest it grows under conifers, but in other areas it may appear under hardwoods and in sagebrush areas of the Great Basin.

Remarks. A beautiful mushroom when well developed, with its petal-like lobes and violet lining of the cup. It seems partial to sandy soil under pines along the eastern slope of the Cascade Mountains. As an edible mushroom it leaves something to be desired; it is definitely poisonous to some persons, and it is difficult to rid of the soil that clings to the outer surface.

Oregon white truffle   *Tuber gibbosum*

OREGON WHITE TRUFFLE (Edible)
Tuber gibbosum (yellowish brown spore mass)

Color and Description

Fruit Body: about .5–2 inches wide, nearly round or irregularly shaped, like a small potato, totally or partially underground; surface light buff to light brown mottled with purplish brown, minutely roughened and matted; interior purple-brown to brick red marbled with white.

When and Where Found. From California to British Columbia, collected almost year-round depending on location and weather conditions. Often under Douglas fir, also in mixed woods and in oak woods.

Remarks. This is a close relative of the edible and highly prized truffles of Europe. It is reported as an excellent edible, similar to the European white truffle, *Tuber magnatum*. In western North America there are a number of truffles (the genus *Tuber* and relatives) and also false truffles (such as the genus *Rhizopogon*). Identification of the species in both groups is difficult and this is the major problem in using this fine edible for the table. But there is a growing interest in truffling in western North America and the future looks bright for enthusiasts. To learn more about these fascinating fungi join a truffling society.

EARLY FALSE MOREL (Edible with caution)
Verpa bohemica (pale yellow spores)

Color and Description

Cap: tan or brown, conspicuously wrinkled, thimble shaped, hollow, lobed edge free from the stem, 1–2 inches wide.

Stem: cream white, long, hollow, often larger at base, 3–5 inches long.

When and Where Found. Early spring, March through April, before the ordinary morel appears. It grows on the ground, often along riverbanks under cottonwoods, willows, and aspens, often well hidden under dead leaves.

Remarks. A widely known fungus that should be eaten with caution. It is poisonous to some individuals, causing loss of muscular coordination and gastrointestinal upset. Others seem to eat it without ill effects. It should not be consumed in large quantities or over several days, and parboiling is recommended since a gyromytrin-like toxin may be produced by this fungus. It is also called the wrinkled thimble-cap or early morel; another scientific name is *Ptychoverpa bohemica*. The bell morel or smooth thimble-cap, *Verpa conica,* also occurs in the west but is infrequent. It has a brownish, somewhat smooth, cone-shaped or thimble-shaped cap on a whitish stalk. The half-free morel, *Morchella semilibera,* is similar in appearance to the early morel. The half-free morel has a yellow-brown skirtlike, honeycombed cap on a whitish stalk. The cap is attached to the stalk for about half its length and the ridges often become darker than the pits. This species occurs in conifer, cottonwood, and alder stands and is widespread but apparently is not so common in the Pacific Northwest. See also species of *Morchella*.

Early false morel   *Verpa bohemica*

Mushroom Poisons

by VARRO E. TYLER

Only 1 to 2 percent of the approximately five thousand species of mushrooms growing in North America are significantly toxic. Still, the types of poisons in this limited number are extremely variable. In recent years much accurate and interesting information on the chemistry and distribution of mushroom poisons has been obtained, and some authors prefer to classify poisonous mushrooms on the basis of the chemistry of their toxic principles. For a general work of this sort, it seems most useful to classify them according to the nature of the effects they produce when eaten by human beings.

Four basic types of mushroom toxins are generally recognized: (1) protoplasmic poisons, (2) compounds affecting the nervous system, (3) gastrointestinal irritants, and (4) coprine (disulfiram-like activity). There are several subvarieties of the first three types. This simple classification does not include poisonings resulting from hypersensitivity (allergy) to mushroom protein or from the ingestion of mushrooms that have been decomposed by microbial action.

The classification scheme also does not include toxicity resulting from potentially hazardous substances that may have accidentally contaminated the fruit bodies. Fortunately, studies with insecticides and fungicides commonly used on cultivated mushrooms have shown that high concentrations of poisonous residues in the fruit bodies are very uncommon and would not ordinarily pose a hazard to health. Of course, it is unwise to collect wild mushrooms from areas where pesticides have been applied recently. All collections, from any location, should be washed thoroughly before eating.

Certain mushrooms also have the ability to accumulate toxic heavy metals from the soil. These metals, such as cadmium and mercury, are actually protoplasmic poisons and might properly be discussed under that heading. However, because they are not mushroom poisons but are, instead, poisons that have found their way into mushrooms, they are considered in a separate category and viewed in a slightly different manner than the other toxins.

All of the known poisonous mushrooms contain principles that produce one or more of the four basic types of effects. However, the observed results are often complicated by differences in concentration of the poisonous principles in different collections of the same species, by the variation in response of different individuals to the same toxin, and by the fact that the mixture of species often consumed at one time by the inexperienced mushroom hunter may contain two or more different types of poisons. One may mask the typical symptoms of another. For example, a mushroom producing a gastrointestinal disturbance of rapid onset would certainly confound the typical symptoms of amatoxin poisoning, which characteristically are delayed at least 6 to 8 hours, if the two mushrooms had been eaten at the same time.

PROTOPLASMIC POISONS

Three basic kinds of protoplasmic poisons are known. All are of significance in this country. Toxic levels of the so-called amanita toxins, or amatoxins, occur in certain species of *Amanita, Galerina, Lepiota,* and *Conocybe*. Another active group of toxins, designated gyromitrins, is found in various *Gyromitra* species. The third type is orellanine, a collective name referring to a group of nephrotoxins (poisons affecting the kidneys) occurring in certain species of *Cortinarius*. Recently, it has been recognized that much, if not all, of the toxicity previously attributed to orellanine is actually due to two components, designated Cortinarin A and Cortinarin B. The latter is especially poisonous. Species containing Cortinarin B most likely occur in the United States; for example, *Cortinarius rainierensis* in the Pacific Northwest is most surely toxic.

Amatoxins

Amatoxins include about half a dozen different cyclopeptides that occur in quantity in a closely related group of *Amanita* species that includes *A. phalloides, A. verna, A. virosa, A. ocreata,* and *A. bisporigera*. These are often called the deadly amanitas. Mushrooms of this group are not common in the Pacific Northwest, but they do occur here. There are indications that some of the species were introduced into the area on the roots of trees with which they form mycorrhizal associations; others are native to this area. *Lepiota helveola, L. josserandii,* and related species also are extremely dangerous, with at least two poisonings in recent years on the Pacific Coast. Dangerous amounts of amatoxins also occur in *Galerina autumnalis, G. marginata,* and *G. venenata.* These species grow with some frequency in Washington and Oregon, but since they are relatively small and nondescript in appearance, they are seldom collected for table use. However, they may be confused with hallucinogenic species of *Psilocybe* by the amateur thrill-seeker. Cases of poisoning resulting in hospitalization and even death have resulted from such confusion. *Conocybe filaris,* a common amatoxin-containing species in our area, also may be confused with hallucinogenic species.

Using very sensitive analytical methods, investigators have been able to detect extremely small amounts of amatoxins in a large number of unrelated species of wild mushrooms. Included were some, such as *Boletus edulis* and *Cantharellus cibarius,* that have long been considered our finest edible varieties. The present consensus among toxicologists is that the presence of such minute amounts of toxins does not render these mushrooms unsafe for consumption.

Poisoning by mushrooms containing large amounts of amatoxins is of the worst type, being insidious in onset and commonly fatal. It is characterized by a long latent period between the eating of the mushrooms and the appearance of symptoms. Ordinarily, 6 to as many as 24 hours will pass; then, abruptly, violent vomiting and diarrhea begin, and may continue until death results. The patient may survive this phase, with appropriate treatment, only to relapse after a day or two because of progressive injury to the liver, kidneys, heart, and central nervous system. In about 30 percent of the cases, death results in 4 to 8 days.

Authorities agree that there is presently no definitive treatment for poisoning by mushrooms containing amatoxins. Persons suspected of having eaten them should be hospitalized immediately, under the direct supervision of a knowledgeable physician. Treatment consists of removal of the toxic material from the digestive tract by administration of emetics (ipecac syrup) and cathartics, gastric lavage, and enemas. Activated charcoal given orally or by nasogastric tube every 3 to 4 hours for at least 24 hours is also helpful. Analgesics may be necessary to control pain, intravenous infusions of liquid to control dehydration and shock, hemodialysis or hemoperfusion to eliminate the toxins. Steps should be taken to maintain a brisk urine flow for the same reason. Additional recommended measures are largely symptomatic and supportive.

Some success has been reported with the use of intravenous corticosteroids to inhibit toxin fixation in the liver, intravenous penicillin G to protect the liver, and intravenous thioctic acid (α-lipoic acid) for the same purpose. Even liver transplantation has been employed. The utility of such measures remains controversial, and application of them should be made only after a careful evaluation of the individual case.

Gyromitrins

Gyromitrin and several closely related compounds, known collectively as the gyromitrins, constitute a second major type of protoplasmic poison. They are less dangerous than the amatoxins but still are potentially fatal. Chemically, the toxins are derivatives of N-methyl-N- formylhydrazine (MFH), which is released in the body and then oxidized to produce the extremely poisonous N-nitroso-N-methylformamide (NMFA). The gyromitrins occur in certain false morels, especially *Gyromitra esculenta* but also in *G. gigas, G. fastigiata* (= *G. brunnea*), *G. infula,* and others. False morels can be rendered edible by parboiling and discarding the water or by long drying; both of these procedures destroy more than 99 percent of the hydrazine content.

There is a singularly irregular distribution of toxicity among different collections of the same species. European specimens of *Gyromitra esculenta* are almost uniformly toxic unless first parboiled or dried, and cases of poisoning from the specimens collected in the eastern United States also are recorded. However, only an occasional case of poisoning has been reported from samples collected west of the Rocky Mountains. Unpublished studies carried out at Purdue University show that the European specimens contain nearly ten times as much gyromitrin as similar specimens collected in the Puget Sound area. Obviously, different races of the species exist, with marked differences in the proportions of their poisonous constituents.

Severe, even fatal, cases of poisoning may arise from eating false morels. As with amatoxins, there is a distinct, although somewhat shorter, latent period between the meal and the onset of symptoms. The period is rarely less than 2 hours, customarily 6 or 8, but may be as long as 20 hours. Symptoms begin with a feeling of fullness in the stomach followed by violent vomiting and watery diarrhea which may persist for one or two days. Headache, lassitude, cramps, and intense pain in the liver and gastric region are followed by jaundice. In severe cases, the patient undergoes general collapse, the pulse becomes irregular, breathing is difficult, and delirium and convulsions occur. Death results in between 15 to 35 percent of cases from liver damage or heart failure, usually within 7 days.

Call a physician in any case of poisoning or suspected poisoning by false morels. Treatment involves intravenous administration of large doses of pyridoxine hydrochloride but otherwise is similar to that recommended for amatoxin poisoning, including emetics or gastric lavage, analgesics, intravenous infusions, and possibly peritoneal dialysis, hemodialysis, or hemoperfusion, with other generally symptomatic and supportive measures.

One final word of caution regarding gyromitrin-containing mushrooms is in order. NMFA, the active principle derived from gyromitrin, has been shown to be highly carcinogenic in small animals. This calls into question the wisdom of eating mushrooms containing even small amounts of gyromitrin, such as Pacific Northwest *Gyromitra esculenta,* or even specimens of this species collected elsewhere, that are high in gyromitrin but have been parboiled or dried to remove the poisonous principles. Although the risk may seem minimal, prudent persons may choose to avoid comsumption of false morels, especially when so many other fine, edible species abound.

Orellanine (Cortinarin A and B)

The third type of protoplasmic poisoning is that produced by orellanine, the mixture of compounds contained in certain *Cortinarius* species. It has only recently been found that two toxic cyclopeptides, designated Cortinarin A and B, closely related chemically to some of the amanita toxins, are the responsible constituents. They apparently account for much, if not all, of the mushrooms' poisonous nature. Both cause serious damage to the kidneys, with Cortinarin B being the more toxic of the two.

Only three species of *Cortinarius, C. orellanus* (from which orellanine was originally obtained), *C. orellanoides,* and *C. speciosissimus,* have thus far been found to contain Cortinarin B, but more than 60 species of the genus contain varying amounts of Cortinarin A. The three deadly species which contain Cortinarin B have not been found in North America for certain. However, there is a possibility that they may occur on this continent. *Cortinarius rainierensis,* a species in the Pacific Northwest, contains orellanine and can be considered toxic. Interestingly, a species found to contain no Cortinarin A or B was *C. violaceus,* one of the few members of the genus considered edible, if not tasty. It now seems prudent to avoid eating any species of *Cortinarius* unless it is proven to be devoid of Cortinarin A and B.

Poisoning by *Cortinarius* toxins is characterized by a very long latent period. Three to 14 days may elapse between the time the mushroom is eaten and appearance of the first symptoms. Then intense, burning thirst is noted, followed by gastrointestinal disturbances, headache, pain in the limbs, spasms, and loss of consciousness. Liver and, particularly, kidney damage result, and death may occur after several weeks or longer. Recovery in less severe cases requires weeks or months. About 15 percent of the reported cases were fatal.

No specific therapy is known. Treatment should emphasize symptomatic relief and maintenance of kidney function.

SUBSTANCES AFFECTING THE NERVOUS SYSTEM

The compounds in mushrooms that have an effect on some portion of the nervous system may be classified into three chemical types: muscarine, ibotenic acid–muscimol, and psilocybin-psilocin. The latter two influence the central nervous system, producing various effects, including hallucinations. Muscarine does not produce such symptoms, its action on the nervous system being strictly peripheral.

Muscarine

First isolated from *Amanita muscaria* in 1869, muscarine derives its name from that species. It does occur in both *A. muscaria* and *A. pantherina* in relatively small amounts, but contrary to some older statements, it is not the principal toxic agent in those mushrooms. Certain species of *Clitocybe,* such as *C. dealbata* and a large number of species of *Inocybe,* including *I. napipes, I. mixtilis,* and *I. pudica,* contain muscarine in considerable quantities and produce cases of poisoning with typical uncomplicated muscarinic symptoms.

These symptoms appear quite soon after the mushrooms have been eaten, usually within 15 to 30 minutes, beginning with greatly increased secretion of saliva, sweat, and tears followed by severe vomiting and diarrhea. Concomitant symptoms are visual disturbances caused by constriction of the pupils, an irregular, slow pulse rate, decreasing blood pressure, and asthmatic breathing. The patient does not experience delirium or hallucinations; mental processes are clear. In severe cases, death infrequently results from paralysis of the heart or respiratory failure; extreme dehydration and electrolyte imbalance are frequently seen in such cases.

Call a physician immediately. Treatment of muscarine poisoning involves lavage of the patient's stomach (unless this has been rendered unnecessary by the vomiting and diarrhea) and the hypodermic administration of atropine sulfate, a specific antidote. After vomiting has ceased, dilute saline solutions and glucose should be administered orally in large amounts. Fatalities occur in about 6 to 12 percent of cases, usually in children or in persons suffering from cardiac or pulmonary disease.

Ibotenic Acid–Muscimol

The symptoms observed in cases of poisoning resulting from the eating of *Amanita muscaria* (fly agaric) and *A. pantherina* (panther amanita) are due to ibotenic acid and muscimol, two closely related compounds which have similar activities and may therefore be considered an entity. Before these compounds were identified, the designation pilzatropine was applied to the toxic principles in these species, since their activity is similar to atropine in certain respects. The term is commonly found in older books on mycology and toxicology.

An additional confusing element is the occurrence of muscarine in both these species and the fact that in the past it has been erroneously designated as the main toxic agent in them. Muscarine does occur in both *Amanita muscaria* and *A. pantherina,* but only in very small amounts, so that the principal effects of poisoning are those of ibotenic acid–muscimol. This is the most common type of mushroom poisoning occurring in the Pacific Northwest, and every collector should be familiar with the symptoms and their treatment.

Symptoms usually appear within 30 minutes to 2 hours after the mushrooms have been eaten. After a brief period of drowsiness, the patient passes into a state of excitement resembling alcoholic intoxication, which may last for 4 hours or more, characterized by confusion, pronounced muscle spasms, delirium, hallucinations, and disturbances of vision. The patient then passes into a deep sleep and later awakes with little or no memory of this excited state. Vomiting occurs only infrequently. Death seldom results and recovery is very rapid, usually within 24 hours.

In cases of poisoning of this type, call a physician. The toxic material must be removed from the gastrointestinal tract. Administration of phenothiazine tranquilizers may help end the excitement and hallucinations; however, because of uncertain interactions, it is probably best to avoid the use of drugs in treatment of this kind of poisoning. Further treatment is largely symptomatic.

It is interesting to note that explorers and travelers who toured Siberia in the early part of the eighteenth century often noted the use of the fly agaric as a narcotic or intoxicant by the Koryak and neighboring tribes of Kamchatka. Vivid descriptions of orgies resulting from the use of this mushroom are recorded in the literature.

Psilocybin-Psilocin

Ingestion of certain small mushrooms not commonly collected for food can cause hallucinations that are particularly vivid and dramatic. Some species of *Psilocybe* and *Conocybe* have been used as intoxicants for many years by Indians in southern Mexico in their medico-religious ceremonies. Certain species or strains of *Panaeolus* produce similar effects. Mushrooms of this type that are most likely to be encountered in the Pacific Northwest are *Conocybe cyanopus, Psilocybe baeocystis, P. cyanescens, P. pelliculosa, P. semilanceata,* and *P. stuntzii,* among others. Certain large species of *Gymnopilus* occurring in the Pacific Northwest such as *G. spectabilis,* also can be hallucinogenic. Two closely related active principles, psilocybin and psilocin, are present in these mushrooms. The former is usually present in larger quantities, but the two have identical physiological actions. These compounds have also been found in *Pluteus salicinus,* but no intoxications by this mushroom are known to date.

First effects are noted half an hour to an hour after eating the mushrooms and continue for several hours. The patient displays anxiety and difficulty in concentrating and understanding. Sensitivity to touch, and changes in size, shape, color, and depth of vision are also experienced. Mood is altered; the patient usually feels elated but may be depressed. Also very common are elementary hallucinations, such as seeing colored lights and patterns when the eyes are closed, and true hallucinations, including changes in perception of the size, weight, and shape of the body.

If a person displays these symptoms after eating mushrooms, call a physician, who will administer symptomatic treatment. In serious cases, chlorpromazine or diazepam may be given to control the untoward effects. Alcohol is frequently consumed along with these mushrooms; its effects may complicate corrective therapeutic measures. Recovery is ordinarily rapid and complete.

GASTROINTESTINAL IRRITANTS

A number of different mushrooms have irritating effects upon the digestive system. Included among these are certain acrid species of *Russula* (for example, *R. emetica* and relatives) and *Lactarius* (the *L. torminosus* group is an example), certain *Boletus* (*B. pulcherrimus*), as well as *Tricholoma pardinum, Entoloma lividum, Hebeloma crustuliniforme, Paxillus involutus, Naematoloma fasciculare,* and *Gomphus floccosus.* Eating them will result in vomiting and mild to extremely severe diarrhea accompanied by abdominal cramps. In most cases, the symptoms end spontaneously within a short period of time, and the patient's health is completely restored in a day or two. *Naematoloma fasciculare, Paxillus involutus, Tricholoma pardinum,* and *Entoloma lividum* are perhaps the most dangerous of all the mushrooms in this category. All are known to have caused deaths, especially in children and elderly persons, or severe illness.

In addition to causing gastric upsets, *Paxillus involutus* may produce serious allergic manifestations, including hemolytic anemia, shock, and kidney failure, in sensitized individuals. A relatively large number of such allergic reactions have been reported since this was first observed in 1971. The condition is insidious in that hypersensitization can occur suddenly after years of eating the mushroom with no untoward effects.

Call a physician in all cases of poisoning by mushrooms containing gastrointestinal irritants. After the toxic material is removed from the digestive tract, bed rest and proper diet are indicated. Serious allergic reactions caused by *Paxillus involutus* require hospitalization and treatment by a knowledgeable physician.

COPRINE

Coprinus atramentarius, the alcohol inky cap, does not produce toxic effects when it is eaten by itself. However, when consumed with alcohol, or when alcohol is consumed even several days later, it produces symptoms in many persons resembling the so-called alcohol-disulfiram syndrome.

Disulfiram is a synthetic drug that is given to chronic alcoholics to discourage them from drinking. If an alcoholic beverage is consumed after disulfiram has been taken, the patient becomes very ill. Symptoms begin in 5 to 10 minutes. The face feels hot and sweaty and becomes flushed to a purple-red color. This condition spreads rapidly over the neck and chest, breathing becomes rapid and difficult, the heart beats rapidly but blood pressure falls, and the patient experiences a violent headache, nausea, vomiting, and great general discomfort. These symptoms last a few hours and are followed by drowsiness and sleep.

The active principle in *Coprinus atramentarius* and related species is not disulfiram but coprine, a unique cyclopropyl amino-acid derivative that is converted in the body to cyclopropanone. This, in turn, interferes with the metabolism of ethyl alcohol in the liver to produce toxic effects similar to those caused by disulfiram. With the mushroom, the latent period is usually somewhat longer; symptoms arise approximately 30 minutes following consumption of alcohol. The severity of poisoning will vary according to the amount of mushroom eaten, the quantity of alcohol consumed, and the time interval between the two. Apparently, there are also individual differences in sensitivity to the effects of coprine.

To be safe, do not eat the mushroom if you have consumed alcohol recently enough for any to remain in the blood stream (i.e., within 24 hours) and then, after the meal, refrain from drinking any alcoholic beverage, even beer or wine, for 5 days. Fortunately, the related species *Coprinus comatus*, the shaggy mane, which is noted for its excellent flavor, does not contain coprine and may be consumed along with alcoholic beverages, if desired.

If poisoning occurs, call a physician. Recovery is usually spontaneous and complete within 2 to 4 hours. Severe cases may require symptomatic and supportive treatment in the form of propanalol for cardiac arrythmias and isotonic fluids or even vasopressor drugs for associated hypotension.

TOXIC HEAVY METALS

In recent years, considerable concern has arisen regarding the ability of certain wild mushrooms, including some favorite edible species, to accumulate toxic heavy metals. Much research has been carried out on this topic, and we now have sufficient knowledge of the scope of the problem to permit establishment of general guidelines, and a few specific rules, for the prudent collector.

Lead and thallium concentrations in wild mushrooms collected in uncontaminated areas are not toxicologically significant. Cadmium and mercury, on the other hand, are accumulated in sufficient amounts by certain species, even when those species grow in relatively unpolluted areas, to present a problem if they are eaten with any frequency.

Some common species which accumulate more than 50 mg of cadmium per kilogram of dry weight under these conditions include *Agaricus arvensis, A. augustus,* and *A. campestris.* A meal of half a pound of such mushrooms would contain nearly 5 times the amount of cadmium generally considered as safe for consumption during an entire week.

Species which accumulate appreciable amounts of mercury even when grown in uncontaminated areas also include some fine edible species. Those with concentrations of more than 10 mg of mercury per kilogram of dry weight include *Agarius arvensis, A. campestris, Boletus edulis, Calvatia gigantea, Lepista nuda,* and *Marasmius oreades.* Less than three-quarters of a pound of these would contain an amount of mercury generally considered as maximal for consumption in a one-week period. Keep in mind, however, that the *Agaricus* species accumulate both cadmium and mercury. Further, if mushrooms grow in areas contaminated by large amounts of toxic heavy metals, the consequences of eating large quantities could be serious; this also applies to species not generally considered heavy-metal accumulators.

How does the dedicated pothunter avoid heavy-metal poisoning and still enjoy the foray and the taste of these woodland delicacies? Here are a few simple rules.

Avoid collecting mushrooms along busy highways or on lawns adjacent to heavily traveled city streets. In such areas, there are increased amounts of lead and mercury from exhaust fumes and of cadmium from tires.

Avoid collecting near mines, smelters, metal refining plants, electroplating facilities, coal-fired generating plants, large garbage or refuse incinerators, and the like. These are often areas of increased contamination with cadmium and mercury as well as lead and thallium.

Avoid frequent meals of mushrooms known to be cadmium or mercury accumulators. If you must eat those species, remove the gills (or, in the case of boletes, the tubes) before cooking. The highest concentrations of heavy metals are found in these tissues.

Frequent consumers of such wild mushrooms should limit their dietary intake of other foods liable to contain high concentration of metallic contaminants; these include liver, kidneys, and fish. They should also avoid smoking, since the cadmium in tobacco smoke is absorbed very readily through the lungs.

Finally, avoid eating too many wild mushrooms of any kind too frequently. Health authorities in Germany recommend limiting consumption of them to half a pound per week. But don't panic! Remember that certain mushrooms grown in unpolluted habitats have always accumulated cadmium and mercury from the soil, and people have eaten them for years with apparent impunity. Still, heavy metals do tend to accumulate in the human system and may eventually reach toxic levels. Be prudent and enjoy these delicacies in moderation, just as is done with many of the finer things of life.

The Hunt, the Quarry, and the Skillet

by ANGELO M. PELLEGRINI

Having read this book, you are now familiar with the mushroom kingdom. You have learned to distinguish the edible from the poisonous species. Where you are uncertain, you will tread with care. You have gathered some mushrooms; and perhaps you have already designated some species of the edible as your favorites. You are becoming acquainted with the several mushroom areas in your region. And now, thinking of the seasons to come, you visualize yourself returning from those areas with baskets filled with your preferred species.

Along the way, your interest in mushrooms has grown. What was once a curiosity, an interesting phenomenon of nature, you now regard as a food of exquisite taste; and you are beginning to search for ways to enjoy completely the expected harvests. Your problem may be put in these terms: What are some of the ways to manage in the kitchen, for immediate and for later use, the mushrooms gathered in the hills and in the meadows? The answer to this question is the subject of these notes.

Let us proceed with this fiction: You have come to my kitchen with a basket of mushrooms you found in the country. You ask me whether I know the variety, and I immediately recognize it as the meadow mushroom, one of the most savory of all the edible species. You tell me—foolishly, as I shall show later!—precisely where you found them. The time is early June.

You offer to share your treasure with me, and we talk about mushrooms and mushroom cookery. I take from the basket one of the smaller meadow mushrooms, a solid little ball with the cap still tightly closed, clean it with a napkin, and pop it into my mouth. You are surprised, even a little frightened, as if I had done something dangerous. Wild mushrooms are suspect among people who know little about them, and the eating of a raw wild mushroom seems a little foolhardy. However, impressed by the apparent relish with which I am eating the mushroom, you ask whether the meadow mushroom is actually good raw.

I reply that practically all edible mushrooms are good raw, some more so than others. Certain cup fungi and many of the helvellas and their relatives should not be eaten uncooked, and some people have a bad reaction to eating raw morels. What I mean to emphasize is that the *taste* of the raw mushroom is generally good and pleasant; and it differs from that of the cooked mushroom. This, as you well know, is also true of many vegetables. Thus, in order to taste all the goodness of a mushroom, to explore it fully as a fine food, one ought to eat it raw as well as cooked.

When I ate that mushroom right from your basket, I was being mischievous. One needs some condiment with the raw mushroom, if only a sprinkling of salt. Since you say you are willing to try, I want to make your first experience with raw wild mushrooms as pleasant as I know how. I propose to make for you a raw wild mushroom spread to be eaten on thin slices of good bread. Observe with care; then we shall eat together.

Let us clean six of the smaller mushrooms and peel two shallots. We now mince these together until the shallot-mushroom mixture is about the consistency of ground meat. From my herb garden I take sprigs of parsley and *Mentha pulegium,* commonly known as English pennyroyal. These are minced separately. Half of the mushroom-shallot mixture is put into a small bowl together with a teaspoon of the minced parsley; the other half is put into another bowl with a teaspoon of the minced pennyroyal. Into each bowl we pour a tablespoon of olive oil and a teaspoon of lemon juice. A dash of salt, a sprinkling of pepper, the ingredients thoroughly mixed, and the two are ready. We spread one on two thin slices of bread, lightly toasted, and the other on two other slices. And these we now eat; first the one, and then the other.

You search for superlatives to express your gratification. These spreads are delicious; and you are now convinced that raw wild mushrooms, with an appropriate condiment, taste good. Think now of what we have done as but a raw mushroom theme on which we can play several variations. We have herbs in the garden, spices in the kitchen cabinet, wine in the cellar, and mushrooms in the basket. All we need in order to work out some variations is a culinary imagination and a bit of gluttony in our makeup.

You noted, did you not, the striking difference between the spread flavored with parsley and the one flavored with pennyroyal? To vary further the basic recipe we may substitute garlic for shallots, and the other fresh herbs such as tarragon, marjoram, or oregano for the two we have used. Or we may combine several herbs. We may top the spread with paper-thin slices of tomato or avocado. Or why not with a good jack cheese? I have some. Why don't we experiment with the cheese?

We prepare enough of the parsley-flavored spread to cover four slices of bread. We arrange on each a few shreds of the jack cheese and place them under the broiler. While the cheese is melting, I pull the cork from a bottle of Chardonnay; when the broiler has done its work, we eat the spread and sip the wine.

Marvelous! And why not? Quality ingredients were properly put together, and the result is gratifying.

Of course, as you suggest, shallots are expensive, and I happen to have the necessary fresh herbs in my garden. But what about people who have neither? Well, you may substitute green onions or chives for shallots, and dried herbs for fresh ones. But remember that a substitute is no more than a substitute. For example, note how little of the aroma of fresh-picked basil remains in the dried herb from the spice cabinet. These aromatic plants are the very soul of cookery, and you need not be without them. Build yourself a garden and grow your own. It is not beyond your competence, and it is a labor of love. You will find all you need to know, in order thus to enrich yourself, in my book *The Food Lover's Garden*.

And now, back to our theme. Can you suggest further variations? Draw on your kitchen experience; put your culinary imagination to work. We began with a mixture of minced mushrooms, shallots, and an herb. Where can we go from here?

Why not cook the spreads we have made? Any one of them, sautéed in a bit of butter or olive oil—I often prefer a mixture of the two—can be used as a base for a mushroom sauce. For example, I have two lamb chops. We shall make a sauce for them in this way. First, I press a little garlic on the lamb chops, season them with salt and pepper, and put them under the broiler. Now, in a bit of butter and oil, in a small skillet, over low heat, I sauté the mushroom mixture flavored with pennyroyal, using only three of the medium- sized mushrooms. Note that the heat is low and the process unhurried, for we must avoid browning or burning the ingredients. Now I stir in a pinch of flour as a thickening agent; then a quarter of a cup of dry vermouth and a teaspoon of lemon juice, stirring as necessary. When the lemon-vermouth is reduced by half, I add enough stock to produce a fluid but thickish sauce. A slow simmer for a few minutes, and the sauce is done. The lamb chops are now broiled. I take them from the broiler, spread the sauce over them, and put them back under the broiler for about a minute.

We eat them, sizzling hot and nicely aromatized. The Chardonnay was grown especially to accompany these chops. Or so we think; and that's all that matters. You agree that lamb chops thus sophisticated belong in the category of transcendental gastronomy.

Now you are probably wondering how this sauce itself may be varied. That is always the proper, the creative mode in the kitchen. Only on rare occasions must one be slavish to a formula. Variations are seldom created in the abstract. They are normally inspired by necessity, by one's gastronomic mood, the intensity of one's appetite, the materials one has on hand. Hence the importance of a well-stocked pantry and fresh herbs in the garden. How often have I conceived a recipe in the garden while garden labor burned calories and gave edge to the appetite and I surveyed what I had grown on my tiny patch of land! In preparing this mushroom sauce we could achieve something different and equally good by using other herbs, by adding cream, or tomato, or a dash of Tabasco for piquancy. That slight suggestion of peppery fire always adds zest to a morsel and makes it more appetizing.

However, one must always use prudence and restraint in experimenting with such ingredients. Too much fat—butter, oil, cream—recoils on its own too much; it tends to cloy on the educated palate. The flavor of the mushroom must not be overwhelmed, as it often is in restaurants, with too much tomato or too heavy a brown sauce. The spreads we made were nicely balanced. Too much of the herbs or lemon juice would have produced less gratifying results.

We could have used this Chardonnay we are enjoying, or any good dry, white wine, instead of the vermouth in making the sauce. I often use it, though I prefer the dry vermouth because of the aromatics in its composition.

You ask whether I have a favorite recipe for cooking mushrooms, and how I intend to prepare these meadow mushrooms that you have brought me.

Not in any particularly sophisticated way. After many years of experimentation in the kitchen, I have come to the conclusion that labored refinement and sophistication do not necessarily yield happy results. In order to achieve fine mushroom cookery, little needs to be added to the butter and olive oil but a crush of garlic and a mince of an herb or two. Tomorrow I shall probably cook the meadow mushrooms in the following way. Slice them. Heat equal parts of olive oil and butter, a generous tablespoon of each for a pound of mushrooms— more if one likes fat and has no fear of it. When it is hot, drop in two cloves of garlic coarsely chopped, a tablespoon of minced parsley, and a teaspoon of minced pennyroyal. When these begin to sizzle in the skillet—and remember not to let them brown or burn!—add the mushrooms, stir briskly, sprinkle with salt and pepper, reduce the heat, and let them cook slowly. That is all.

I have mentioned some of the herbs that may be used. There is another highly recommended by Italian chefs. It is *Nepeta cataria,* catnip or catmint. The Italian name, *nepitella,* is more attractive. Others prefer oregano and call it *erba da funghi,* mushroom grass. The flavor of these herbs harmonizes with that of mushrooms and accentuates it. They both yield excellent results, and either can be used with the indispensable parsley. And mushrooms cooked in this way suggest any number of variations.

To make an excellent mushroom sauce, one may add a liquid— either wine, stock, cream, or tomato. And this reminds me of a dish I must tell you about. Let us simply call it rabbit or fowl, preferably game fowl, to be cooked with mushrooms and eaten with polenta or rice. It is a gluttony burgher's dish, one that generates heat and creates energy—a dish that is therefore appropriate for the fall and winter. In this dish, the wild mushroom is not cooked for its own sake, as a dish in itself; it is used as an auxiliary food, a flavoring ingredient, though easily the star of such ingredients. And, indeed in all high-level cuisine the mushroom is used more often as a supporting element than as a central one; but the support it gives is actually what gives distinction to the star.

And so it is with—shall we say rabbit stew with mushrooms? I choose rabbit because it is nearer to game than fowl and easier to come by than game. Cut the rabbit into small pieces, dust them lightly with flour, brown them slowly in olive oil and butter, using salt and pepper to taste. Remove them from the skillet; then sauté the mushrooms, a pound or somewhat more for one rabbit, in the fat and meat juice in the way I have already described. Add half a cup of dry white wine and reduce; add a small tin of tomato sauce and an equal measure of stock. Stir well, simmer briefly, correct for seasoning, and finish cooking the rabbit in the sauce. Serve it with rice; or, much better, with polenta.

You may be among those unfortunate ones who do not know what polenta is. It is nothing more than a thick cornmeal mush. To prepare it, drop half a stick of butter into two quarts of boiling, salted water, then stir in enough coarse-ground yellow cornmeal to produce a heavy, thick, grainy paste as solid as bread dough. Add the cornmeal to the boiling water in driblets, stirring constantly with a large wooden spoon until you have achieved the desired density. Cook it over slow heat for about forty-five minutes. When it is done, upend the kettle on a cutting board and let the polenta slip out. Let it rest for a few minutes until it is firm and can be sliced. Arrange a generous slice on a plate and spoon the rabbit or fowl and mushrooms over it. A bit of grated Parmesan cheese scattered on it will add to your delight.

Rabbit and mushroom stew served this way is a great dish. While eating it, you are thankful that you did not die yesterday. And it is the dedicated mushroom hunter's dish, as much as sourdough pancakes are the prospector's dish. Mate it, of course, with the headiest claret or burgundy you can afford.

Any edible variety of mushroom—boletus, chanterelle, shaggy mane, the prince, whatever the hunt yields—can be used in this manner. And, by the way, if you have never eaten fried *Boletus edulis* with fried artichokes, then there is a gastronomic delight for you to anticipate. Frying is one of the best ways to prepare certain mushrooms for the table, especially boletus, morel, shaggy mane, and the meadow mushroom. Cut them into slices about a third of an inch thick, dust them with flour, dip them into beaten egg, and fry them slowly, until nicely browned, in no more olive oil than is necessary to cover well the bottom of the skillet. Pare small artichokes down to the heart, cut them into slices, and treat them the same way. Salt and pepper to taste, and, just before removing them from the pan, squeeze a few drops of lemon juice on them. Prepared in this way, the *Boletus edulis* becomes a culinary classic.

If you are ever so fortunate as to find yourself with a whole shopping bag full of mushrooms, you may want to freeze some of them. Mushrooms can be frozen without any appreciable loss of texture or taste. For best results cook them completely with all seasonings as you would for the table and then freeze them in well-sealed containers. They will keep without noticeable deterioration for more than a year. One may also sauté the mushrooms, seasoned as one likes, and then reduce them to a paste in a blender using, as needed, slight additions of stock to facilitate the transformation. The paste is then frozen in small containers and used when needed to enrich a sauce.

This mushroom paste can be spread on a steak as it broils, or warmed and spread on a slice of roast beef. In either case one must use it rather sparingly for it is concentrated mushroom and too much of it will humble the taste of the beef. When used to season a steak, whether broiled or pan fried, the heated sauce should be spread on the meat after it is done. A minute is all that is required to achieve a proper integration of meat and sauce. A longer time might burn the sauce or dissipate too much of its moisture.

And now let me tell you that if you have never eaten wild mushroom soup, then you have no idea what a delicacy cream of mushroom soup can be. I made it for the first time several years ago out of sheer desperation. I came home from one of the more grim and determined hunts loaded with morels. We could eat only so many. We had already more than we could use in the freezer. What should we do with these? I thought of mushroom soup—which I like very much but had never made. I consulted the cookbooks, only to discover that only one included a recipe for mushroom soup, and that not a very satisfactory one. So I created my own. I cleaned the morels and cooked them partially in butter and oil with shallots and parsley. Then I creamed them in a blender and finished cooking them in chicken broth, just enough of the broth to yield a dense but nicely fluid soup. The only spice I used was a bit of nutmeg. When the soup had simmered for about fifteen minutes I put it into quart jars. The yield was eight quarts. No flour was used, no filler, no thickening agent. The density and substance of the soup were produced by the abundance of morels. And in that state the soup was frozen. A rich cream, about a cup for each quart, would be added later when the soup was thawed and heated for serving. One might also add a bit of dry sherry, but sherry must never be used unless it is dry and of superior quality.

Needless to say, so-called cooking sherry should never be used. Avoid it as you would the plague! Strictly speaking, there is no such thing as cooking sherry or cooking wine. Wine is either ordinary or superior; and only the latter should be used in fine cuisine. Well! We had the last of those eight quarts two years after the soup was made. We thawed it, heated it, added the cream, and served it to guests who were amazed by the age of the soup and its authentic mushroom richness. Later I made mushroom soup using the meadow mushroom, with excellent results. I made it also on another occasion using boletus. The soup was good, but not so good as the morel soup. On another occasion I combined morels and boletus, with gratifying results. In summary, I would be inclined to say that when one comes home from the hunt groaning under a burden of mushrooms, the most advantageous use of the surplus is to convert it into mushroom soup.

Another recommended method of conserving mushrooms is drying them. Any mushroom can be dried; but the one that can be best treated in this way for culinary purposes is the boletus, preferably the *Boletus edulis*. It is this variety that comes to us dry from the Balkans and the Mediterranean and that is so expensive, as much as forty dollars a pound. It is the one mushroom that has a stronger nose when dried than when fresh; and it is the one dried mushroom that great chefs of the Western world prefer above all others in making certain mushroom-flavored sauces. In our home it has always been preferred to the fresh as an ingredient in the classic spaghetti sauce and in making risotto. A scant handful is all one needs to execute the ordinary household recipe.

The procedure for drying mushrooms is not at all complicated. The mushroom is trimmed and cleaned with a soft brush and a paring knife. It is then cut into slices about a quarter of an inch thick, and these are distributed on a screen such as is used in screening soil, or on one made for the purpose by stretching plastic or metal screening over a rectangular frame. The drying should be accomplished in the sun whenever possible, and for this reason one should dry the mushrooms that are hunted in the late spring, when sunny days are more likely to occur than in the fall. Lacking sun, the drying may be done in a warm, well-ventilated room. Before they are stored in tins, jars, or plastic bags, the mushrooms must be tinder dry. If there is residual moisture, they will generate nasty vermin.

Never wash mushrooms before drying them. Mushrooms are spongy; they absorb water easily, and water thins out their flavor. So, whenever possible, one should cook them without washing them. If they are properly trimmed when they are gathered, especially the root end of the stem, there is very little soil left on them, no more than can be easily removed with a soft brush or moist cloth. When you gathered these meadow mushrooms you failed to trim the stems, so there is considerable dirt strewn among them in the basket, and some of them will have to be washed.

When dried mushrooms are used in cooking—and they are normally used as flavoring agents only—they are first soaked in boiling water, dropped in and stirred for about half a minute in the rolling boil. This frees whatever dirt may be sticking to them. The pan is set aside for a couple of minutes to let dirt particles sink to the bottom; then the mushrooms are lifted with a slotted spoon onto the chopping board. Use no more water than is needed to do the job. When the mushrooms are removed, pour the water carefully off the residue and set it aside. It will be charged with mushroom flavor, and you may want to incorporate some of it into whatever sauce you are making. Remember that this entire process of rendering dried mushrooms soft and pliable requires no more than a couple of minutes. If the mushrooms are left too long in the water, some of the flavor will go down the drain, especially when the water itself is not used.

One more suggestion now regarding the rabbit or fowl dish with mushrooms and polenta. One spring I came home from a mushroom hunt with ten pounds of prime *Boletus edulis*. After we had eaten our fill, I cooked the surplus in the tomato sauce I described for the rabbit recipe and froze it in a number of small containers. The virtue of this procedure is obvious. When you want the rabbit or fowl with mushrooms, brown the meat, add the packet of frozen mushrooms in tomato sauce, pull the cork from a bottle of whatever red wine you prefer, and call the guests to the dinner table.

My final advice to you is that you learn to be a true mushroom hunter—grim, greedy, and cunning—not a sophisticated dilettante. The mushroom hunter does not gather mushrooms or merely pick them. He hunts them down; and as often as not he finds them when they are not there. Let me explain. What I mean is that the passion, the greed, the grim determination, the cunning, the trained nose—all of these combine to give the mushroom hunter such acuity of perception that he can see a mushroom when it is still under the mulch, invisible to others. When stalking the mushroom, he has no other interests, passions, feelings save an insatiable greed for the quarry. He differs from men who hunt and fish. These may be, and often are, abstemious. When the game is in the bag, their excitement is over. Not so the mushroom hunter. He drools as he hunts; and as he lunges his way through the tangle of vine maple among conifers in search of *Boletus edulis*, he plots its fate in the skillet. His consuming passion for mushrooms informs his hunt and makes him relentless in it. It accounts for his effectiveness. Thus we cannot separate the hunt from the enjoyment of the quarry; the process is continuous. What was desire in the hills becomes fulfillment in the kitchen. So don't be a mushroom buff, a mere mycologist whose center of interest is the display room or the laboratory. Aspire to be a hunter whose center of interest is his belly.

As such he has a credo and an eccentricity. He hunts only at the crack of dawn and wears his shirt inside out. To ask why is to ask why fire burns. His credo may be stated thus: He has sworn an oath to keep his mushroom patches a secret and to find and poach on the patches of other hunters. When mushrooms are the prize, the scope of all his aspirations is narrowed to these two goals. Though in all else he may be as saintly as Saint Francis, in the pursuit of these ends he is more satanic than Satan. He will betray his nearest and dearest without the slightest twitch of flesh or spirit. He is amoral.

You told me where you found these meadow mushrooms, in the meadow where road x crosses road y. It was good of you; but it was unpardonable folly. Thanks for your generosity. Now go your way; you are initiated into the tribe of those who have a pagan reverence for mushrooms.

Selected Bibliography

Ammirati, J. F., J. A. Traquair, and P. A. Horgen. *Poisonous Mushrooms of Canada and Other Inedibe Fungi.* Markham, Ont.: Fitzhenry and Whiteside, 1985.

————. *Poisonous Mushrooms of the Northern United States and Canada.* Minneapolis: University of Minnesota Press, 1985.

Arora, D. *Mushrooms Demystified.* Second edition. Berkeley: Ten Speed Press, 1986.

Bandoni, R. J., and A. F. Szczawinski. *Guide to Common Mushrooms of British Columbia.* British Columbia Provincial Museum Handbook No. 24. Victoria, B.C.: A. Sutton, 1964. Revised edition 1976.

Biek, D. *The Mushrooms of Northern California.* Redding: Spore Prints, 1984.

Groves, J. W. *Edible and Poisonous Mushrooms of Canada.* Revised. Ottawa, Ont.: Canada Agriculture, 1975.

Kerrigan, R. W. *The Agaricales of California. Vol. 6, Agaricaceae.* Eureka: Mad River Press, 1987.

Lange, M. and F. B. Hora. *A Guide to Mushrooms and Toadstools.* New York: E. P. Dutton and Co., 1967.

Largent, D. L. *The Agaricales of California. Vol. 5, Hygrophoraceae.* Eureka: Mad River Press, 1985.

Lincoff, G. H. *The Audubon Soceity Field Guide to North American Mushrooms.* New York: A. A. Knopf, Chanticleer Press, 1981.

McKenny, M. *Mushrooms of Field and Wood.* New York: John Day Co., 1929.

Miller, O. K., Jr. *Mushrooms of North America.* Paperback reprint. New York: E. P. Dutton and Co., 1977.

Phillips, R. *Mushrooms and Other Fungi of Great Britain and Europe.* London: Pan Books Ltd., 1981.

Puget Sound Mycological Society. *Wild Mushroom Recipes.* Seattle: Pacific Search Press, 1973.

Smith, A. H. *Mushrooms in Their Natural Habitats.* Portland, Ore.: Sawyers, 1949.

―――. *A Field Guide to Western Mushrooms*. Ann Arbor: University of Michigan Press, 1975.

Smith, A. H., H. V. Smith, and N. S. Weber. *How to Know the Gilled Mushrooms*. Dubuque: Wm. C. Brown, 1979.

―――. *How to Know the Non-Gilled Mushrooms*. Dubuque: Wm. C. Brown, 1981.

Stamets, P. *Psilocybe Musrhooms and Their Allies*. Seattle: Homestead Book Co., 1978.

Thiers, H. D. *California Mushrooms: A Field Guide to the Boletes*. New York: Hafner Publishing Co., 1975.

―――. *The Agaricales of California. Vol. 1, Amanitaceae*. Eureka: Mad River Press, 1982.

―――. *The Agaricales of California. Vol. 2, Cantharellaceae*. Eureka: Mad River Press, 1985.

―――. *The Agaricales of California. Vol. 3, Gomphidiaceae*. Eureka: Mad River Press, 1985.

―――. *The Agaricales of California. Vol. 4, Paxillaceae*. Eureka: Mad River Press, 1985.

Tylutki, E. E. *Mushrooms of Idaho and the Pacific Northwest Discomycetes*. Moscow: University Press of Idaho, 1979.

Index

Admirable boletus, 6-7
Agaricus. 150, 227
  albolutescens. 151
  arvensis. 150, 227
  augustus. 143, 145, 227
  campestris. 144-45, 227
  hondensis. 144, 146
  meleagris. 149
  nivescens, 147
  placomyces, 149
  praeclarisquamosus. 144, 148
  silvaticus. 149-50
  silvicola, 150-51
  subrutilescens. 151
  xanthodermus, 151
Agrocybe
  pediades, 122
  praecox, 121
Alcohol inky cap, 154
Aleuria aurantia, 198-99
Alice Eastwood's boletus, 8-9
Almond-scented russula, 96-97
Almond waxy cap, 60-61
Amanita, 217
  aspera, 32-33
  bisporigera, 217
  calyptrata, 33, 35
  gemmata, 34-35, 166
  muscaria, xiii, 34, 36, 222-23
  ocreata, 36-37, 39, 108, 217
  pantherina. 33-34, 38, 222-23
  phalloides, 37, 39, 217
  porphyria, 40-41
  silvicola, 40-41, 108
  smithiana, 42-43, 108
  vaginata, 43, 120
  verna, xiii, 37, 217
  virosa, 37, 217
Amatoxins, 217-19

Angel's wings, 92-93
Anise-scented clitocybe, 54-55
Apricot jelly mushroom, 186
Armillaria. 108, 113
  albolanaripes. 44
  luteovirens. 44
  mellea. 45
  ponderosum. 107-8
Auricularia
  auricula. 184-85
  polytricha, 184
Autumnal galerina, 128

Beefsteak morel, 203
Bell morel, 214
Bell-shaped panaeolus, 162
Big laughing gymnopilus, 129
Bitter false paxillus, 83-84
Blackening russula, 98-99
Black morel, 208-9
Black-tufted wood tricholoma, 114
Blah coral, 177
Blue-staining boletus, 16
Blue-staining cup, 199-200
Blushing hygrophorus, 66
Blushing inocybe, 134
Boletinus lakei, 19
Boletopsis leucomelaena, 168
Boletus, 224
  aurantiacus, 12
  brevipes, 15
  calopus, 4, 11
  chrysenteron, 2-3, 11
  coniferarum, 4
  eastwoodiae, 9
  edulis, 5, 218, 227, 234-36, 238
  lakei, 19
  luteus, 20
  mirabilis, 6-7

olituceobrunneus, 24
piperatus, 6-8
pulcherrimus, 8-9, 224
rubripes, 11
satanas, 9
smithii, 9-10
zelleri, 10-11
Boone's giant puffball, 190-91
Bovista
  pila, 189-90
  plumbea, 189
Brain mushroom, 201-5
Bristly pholiota, 139-40
Brown dunce cap, 122
Buttery collybia, 56

Calbovista subsculpta, 190-92
California elfin saddle, 201-2
Caloscypha fulgens, 199-200
Calvatia
  booniana, 190-92
  gigantea, 192, 227
  sculpta, 192
Cantharellus, 60
  cibarius, 25, 218
  infundibuliformis, 26-27
  subalbidus, 26-28
  tubaeformis, 27
Capped amanita, 33, 35
Carmine coral, 178
Catathelasma
  imperialis, 46
  ventricosa, 46-47
Cauliflower mushroom, 183
Cep, 5
Changeable melanoleuca, 88-89
Chicken mushroom, 169
Chicken of the wood, 169
Chlorophyllum molybdites, 86
Chroogomphus
  rutilus, 152-53
  tomentosus, 152-53
Clavaria
  purpurea, 174-75
  vermicularis, 174

Clavariadelphus
  borealis, 176
  pistillaris, 176
  truncatus, 174-76
Clavulina cristata, 176
Clean mycena, 89-90
Clitocybe, 222
  albirhiza, 47-48
  avellaneialba, 48-49
  dealbata, 161, 222
  dealbata var. *sudorifica*, 49-50
  dilatata, 51, 85
  inversa, 52
  nebularis, 53
  nuda, 81
  odora var. *pacifica*, 54-55
Clitopilus prunulus, 116
Clustered blue chanterelle, 31
Clustered collybia, 54-55
Clustered woodlover, 160
Collybia
  acervata, 54-55
  butyracea, 56
  dryophila, 56
Colorful gomphidius, 152-53
Comb russula, 101
Common laccaria, 70
Common paxillus, 135
Common scaly-stemmed boletus, 14
Cone-shaped waxy cap, 63
Conifer boletus, 4
Conifer false morel, 203
Conocybe, 217, 223
  cyanopus, 224
  filaris, 122-23, 218
  tenera, 122
Coprine, 225-226
Coprinus
  atramentarius, 154, 225
  comatus, 155, 226
  micaceus, 156-57
Coral hydnum, 170
Cortinarin A and B, 220-21
Cortinarius, 217, 220-21
  mutabilis, 123-24

orellanoides, 221
orellanus, 221
phoeniceus var. occidentalis, 124-25
pyriodorus, 126
rainierensis, 217, 221
semisanguineus, 125
speciosissimus, 221
traganus, 126-27
violaceus, 126-27, 221
Crested coral, 176
Crowded white clitocybe, 51
Cystoderma
  amianthinum, 57-58
  fallax, 58

Dacrymyces palmatus, 184-85
Dark boletus, 24
Dark-centered hebeloma, 131
Deadly conocybe, 122-23, 165
Deadly galerina, 165
Deadly lepiota, 80
Death cup, 37, 39
Deer mushroom, 119
Delicious milky cap, 71, 76
Destroying angel, xiii, 36-37
Discina perlata, 200-201
Dotted-stalked slippery jack, 18

Early false morel, 214-15
Early morel, 214
Edible fake morel, 203
Edible morel, 209-10
Elfin saddle, 206
Emetic russula, 96-97
Entoloma, 85, 116
  lividum, 116-17, 224-25
  sericeum, 118, 161
European white truffle, 213

Fairy ring mushroom, 50, 87
False chanterelle, 58-59
False morel, 203
Felt-ringed agaricus, 146
Fetid russula, 98

Flammulina velutipes, 58-59
Flat-topped coral, 174-75
Flat-topped mushroom, 148, 150
Fly agaric, 223
Fly amanita, xiii, ix, 34, 36
Fried chicken mushroom, 51, 84-85, 118
Funnel-shaped chanterelle, 26
Fuscoboletinus, 12
  ochraceoroseus, 11, 13, 17
Fuzzy-footed coral, 179

Galerina, 217
  autumnalis, 122, 128, 218
  marginata, 218
  venenata, 129, 165, 218
Garlic marasmius, 88
Gastrointestinal irritants, 224-25
Gaestrum saccatum, 193
Gem-studded puffball, 194
Giant helvella, 201-2, 204
Giant puffball, x, 190
Golden false pholiota, 137-38
Gomphidius
  glutinosus, 156
  oregonensis, 156-57
  rutilus, 152-53
  subroseus, 158-59
  tomentosus, 152-53
Gomphus
  clavatus, 28-29
  floccosus, 25, 29-30, 224
  kauffmanii, 30
Graycap, 53
Green-gilled woodlover, 158
Green-spored lepiota, 86
Gymnopilus, 224
  spectabilis, 129, 224
Gypsy mushroom, 142-43
Gyromitra, 217
  ambigua, 205
  brunnea, 219
  californica, 201-2
  esculenta, 202-3, 219-20

fastigiata, 219
gigas, 204, 219
infula, 205, 219
montana, 205
Gyromitrins, 219-20

Half-free morel, 214
Haymaker's mushroom, 161
Heavy metals (toxic), 226-28
Hebeloma
  crustuliniforme, 130, 224
  mesophaeum, 131
Helvella
  esculenta, 203
  gigas, 205
  lacunosa, 206
Hericium abietis, 170
Ho-Elor, 184
Hollow-stalked larch boletus, 17
Honey mushroom, 45
Hooded helvella, 201, 204-5
Hydnellum peckii, 171-72
Hydnum
  repandum, 171-72
  umbilicatum, 173
Hygrocybe
  conica, 63
  miniata, 64-65
Hygrophoropsis aurantiaca, 26, 58-59
Hygrophorus, 62, 68
  agathosmus, 60-61
  bakerensis, 60-61
  calophyllus, 62
  camarophyllus, 62
  conicus, 63
  gliocyclus, 64-65
  hypothejus, 67
  miniatus, 64-65
  pudorinus, 66
  speciosus, 67
  subalpinus, 68-69
Hypomyces lactifluorum, 207

Ibotenic acid, 222-23

Inocybe, 222
  geophylla, 135
  lacera, 132
  lilacina, 135
  mixtilis, 222
  napipes, 133, 222
  pudica, 134, 222

Japanese pine mushroom, 107-8
Jonquil amanita, 34-35

Kauffman's phaeocollybia, 136-37
King boletus, 5, 12, 144
Kurotake, 168

Laccaria
  amethysteo-occidentalis, 68-69
  bicolor, 70
  laccata, 70
Lactarius, 33, 70, 74, 207, 224
  aurantiacus, 72
  deliciosus, 71
  luculentus, 72
  mucidus, 74
  pallescens var. *pallescens*, 73
  pseudomucidus, 74
  pubescens var. *betulae*, 75
  rubrilacteus, 76
  rufus, 77
  sanguifluus, 76
  scrobiculatus var. *canadensis*, 78
  torminosus, 75, 224
  uvidus, 73
Laetiporus sulphureus, 169
Lake's boletus, 16, 19
Langermannia, 192
Larch waxy cap, 67
Late oyster mushroom, 92-93
Lead-colored puffball, 189
Leccinum
  aurantiacum, 12-13
  scabrum, 14
Lemon-yellow pholiota, 138-39, 141
Lepiota, 79, 217

clypeolaria, 79
  helveola, 79-80, 218
  josserandii, 218
  naucina, 82
  rachodes, 86
  rubrotincta, 79
  subincarnata, 80
Lepista nuda, 81, 227
Leucoagaricus naucinus, 82
Leucopaxillus
  albissimus, 83
  albissimus var. albissimus, 83
  albissimus var. lentus, 83
  amarus, 83-84
Liberty cap, 165
Livid entoloma, 117
Lobster mushroom, 207
Lorchel, 203
Lycoperdon
  perlatum, 194
  pyriforme, 194-95
Lyophyllum, 85
  decastes, 84

Macrolepiota rachodes, 86
Man-on-horseback, 104-5
Marasmius
  oreades, 87, 161, 227
  scorodonius, 88
Matsutake, 107-8
Meadow mushroom, x-xiii, 144-45,
  229-30, 233, 235-36, 239
Melanoleuca, 89
  melaleuca, 88-89
Morchella, 214
  angusticeps, 209
  conica, 209
  crassipes, 209-10
  deliciosa, 210
  elata, 208-10
  esculenta, 209-10
  semilibera, 209, 214
Mt. Baker waxy cap, 60-61
Muscarine, 222

Muscimol, 222-23
Mycena, 90
  pura, 89-90
  strobilinoides, 91

Naematoloma
  capnoides, 158-59
  fasiculare, 158, 160, 224-25
Northwest spring coral, 182

Oak-loving collybia, 56
Olive-capped boletus, 20-21
Orange-capped boletus, 12-14
Orange fairy cup, 198-99
Orange funnel-cap, 52
Orange jelly, 184-85, 188
Orange jelly-belly coral, 180-81
Orange milky cap, 72
Oregon gelatinous coral, 180-81
Oregon gomphidius, 156-58
Oregon white truffle, 213
Orellanine, 220-21
Oyster mushroom, 92, 94

Pale-capped violet latex lactarius, 73
Panaeolina foenisecii, 161
Panaeolus, 224
  campanulatus, 162
Panellus serotinus, 92-93
Panther amanita, 33-34, 38
Paxillus involutus, 135, 224-25
Pear-shaped puffball, 194-95
Peck's hydnum, 171-72
Peppery boletus, 6, 8
Peziza, 211
  badia, 211
  praetivisa, 211
  repanda, 211
Phaeocollybia kauffmanii, 136-37
Phaeolepiota aurea, 137-38
Phlogiotis helvelloides, 186
Pholiota
  limonella, 138-39, 141
  squarrosa, 141

squarroso-adiposa, 139
squarrosoides, 140
terrestris, 141
Pholiotina filaris, 122
Pig's ear, 200-201
Pig's ear gomphus, 28-29, 31
Pitted milky cap, 78
Pleurocybella porrigens, 92-93
Pleurotus
    ostreatus, 94
    porrigens, 92-93
Pluteus
    cervinus, 119
    salicinus, 224
Poison pie, 130, 132
Polyozellus multiplex, 31
Polyporus sulphureus, 169
Prairie mushroom, 150
Prince, 143, 145, 150, 234
Protoplasmic poisons, 217-21
Psathyrella longistriata, 163
Pseudohydnum gelatinosum, 187
Psilocin, 223-24
Psilocybe, 122, 129, 218, 223
    baeocystis, 224
    cyanescens, 224
    pelliculosa, 224
    semilanceata, 165, 224
    stuntzii, 122, 129, 164, 224
Psilocybin, 223-24
Ptychoverpa bohemica, 214
Pungent cortinarius, 126-27
Pure cystoderma, 57
Purple-brown amanita, 40, 41
Purple club coral, 174-75
Purple-staining cortinarius, 123-24

Questionable stropharia, 165-66

Ramaria
    acrisiccescens, 177
    araiospora, 178
    araiospora var. rubella, 178
    botrytis, 179

cyaneigranosa, 178
cystidiophora, 179
gelatiniaurantia, 180
gelatinosa var. oregonensis, 181
    magnipes, 182
    rasilispora, 182
    rubripermanens, 178
    sandaracina, 180
    stuntzii, 178
    subbotrytis, 178
Red-brown tricholoma, 106-7
Red-juice milky cap, 76
Red milky cap, 77
Red-orange mycena, 91
Red-tufted wood tricholoma, 115
Rhizopogon, 213
    ellenae, 196
    occidentalis, 195-96
    parksii, 196
Rhodophyllus
    lividus, 117
    sericeus, 118
Ringed psathyrella, 163
Rose coral, 178
Rose-red russula, 102
Rosy gomphidius, 158-59
Rosy larch boletus, 11, 13
Rough-capped hydnum, 173
Rough pholiota, 139
Rounded earthstar, 193
Rozites caperata, 142-43
Russet scaly tricholoma, 112
Russula, 33, 207, 224
    albonigra, 99
    brevipes, 68, 95
    brevipes var. acrior, 96
    cascadensis, 96
    claroflava, 100
    decolorans, 100
    delica, 96
    densifolia, 98
    dissimulans, 99
    emetica, 96-97, 102, 224
    foetens, 98, 101

laurocerasi, 96-98
nigricans, 98-99
occidentalis, 99-100
olivacea, 104
pectinata, 101
rosacea, 96, 102
subnigricans, 99
xerampelina, 102-4
xerampelina var. *elaeodes,* 104

Sandy tricholoma, 109
Sarcodon
  imbricatum, 173
  scabrosum, 173
Sarcosphaera crassa, 212
Scaly hydnum, 173
Scaly pholiota, 141
Scarlet waxy cap, 64-65
Scleroderma, 189, 197
  citrinum, 197
Shaggy lepiota, 86
Shaggy mane, 154-55, 226, 234-35
Shaggy-stalked armillaria, 44
Shaggy-stalked lepiota, 79
Sheathed amanita, 43
Shiny cap, 156-57
Shoestring root rot, 46
Short-stemmed russula, 95
Short-stemmed slippery jack, 15
Showy volvaria, 120
Sierran puffball, 190, 192
Silky entoloma, 118
Slimy gomphidius, 156
Slimy milky cap, 74
Slimy waxy cap, 64-65
Slippery jack, 20-21
Smith's amanita, 42
Smith's boletus, 9-10
Smoky brown clitocybe, 48-49
Smoky-gilled woodlover, 158-60
Smooth thimble-cap, 214
Snowy cap, 147
Soapy tricholoma, 110-11
Sooty brown waxy cap, 62

Sparassis
  crispa, 183
  radicata, 183
Spreading-hedgehog mushroom,
  171-72
Spreading peziza, 211
Spring agrocybe, 121
Steinpilz, 5
Streaked tricholoma, 110-11
Stropharia
  ambigua, 165-66
  rugoso-annulata, 166-67
Stuntz's psilocybe, 164
Subalpine waxy cap, 68-69
Suillus, 12, 15
  americanus, 22
  brevipes, 15, 20
  caerulescens, 16, 19
  cavipes, 12, 17
  granulatus, 18, 20
  lakei, 12, 19
  luteus, 20-22
  punctatipes, 18
  sibiricus, 22
  subolivaceus, 20-21
  tomentosus, 22-23
  umbonatus, 20
Sulfur shelf, 169
Sulfur tuft, 160
Sulphur tricholoma, 104
Sweat-producing clitocybe, 49-50, 87
Sweetbread mushroom, 116
Swollen-stalked catathelasma, 46-47
Sylvan agaricus, 149

Terrestrial pholiota, 141
Thick-skinned puffball, 197
Tiger tricholoma, 105-6
Torn-capped inocybe, 132
Tree-ear, 184-85
Tremella
  lutescens, 188
  mesenterica, 188

Tricholoma
  caligatum, 108
  flavovirens, 104-5
  focale, 113
  imbricatum, 112
  inamoenum, 104
  magnivelare, 108
  nuda, 81
  pardinum, 105-6, 224-25
  personatum, 81
  pessundatum, 106-7, 109, 112
  ponderosum, 107-8
  populinum, 109
  portentosum, 110-11
  saponaceum, 110-11
  vaccinum, 107, 112
  zelleri, 113
Tricholomopsis
  decora, 114
  rutilans, 115
Tuber, 213
  gibbosum, 213
  magnatum, 213
Tumbling puffball, 189-90
Turnip-bulb inocybe, 133
Tylopilus pseudoscaber, 24

Velvet-stemmed flammulina, 58-59
Verpa
  bohemica, 209, 214-15
  conica, 214
Violet cortinarius, 70, 126, 127
Violet star cup, 212
Volvariella speciosa, 120

Warted amanita, 32-33
Warted giant puffball, 190-92
Western cauliflower mushroom, 183
Western giant puffball, 192
Western purple laccaria, 68-70
Western red-capped cortinarius, 124-25
Western rhizopogon, 195-96
Western russula, 99-100

White chanterelle, 27-28
White false paxillus, 83
White jelly mushroom, 187
White lepiota, 82
White morel, 210
White-stranded clitocybe, 47-48
White worm coral, 174
Wine-red stropharica, 166-67
Wine-tipped coral, 179
Witch's butter, 188
Woods blewits, 81
Wood-ear, 184
Woodland amanita, 40-41, 43
Woodland mushroom, 147, 150-51
Woodland russula, 103
Woolly-capped boletus, 22-23
Woolly chanterelle, 26, 29-30
Woolly gomphidius, 152-53
Woolly milky cap, 75
Woolly-stemmed agaricus, 151
Wrinkled thimble cap, 214

Yellow chanterelle, 25-27, 30, 144
Yellow-fleshed boletus, 2-3

Zeller's boletus, 3, 10-11
Zeller's tricholoma, 113

Margaret McKenny was a well-known author, lecturer, and nature photographer who originally conceived and wrote the first edition of this guidebook. Her name is among those most widely recognized by amateur and professional mushroom hunters. Daniel E. Stuntz was professor of botany at the University of Washington. He was responsible for preparing the first revised edition of *The Savory Wild Mushroom* which was published in 1971. Joseph F. Ammirati is professor of botany and adjunct professor of forest resources at the University of Washington. He is a member of the Toxicology Committee of the North American Mycological Association, serves on the editorial board of *Mushroom: The Journal of Wild Mushrooming,* and is coauthor of *Poisonous Mushrooms of the Northern United States and Canada.*